ACQUIRING YOUR FUTURE THROUGH A SUCCESSION PLAN

A Primer for Next Generation
Professional Service Providers

AUTHOR MEMBER

Alliance of
Independent
Authors

DAVID GRAU SR., JD

Acquiring Your Future Through a Succession Plan:
A Primer for Next Generation Professional Service Providers

This publication is designed to provide accurate and authoritative information in regard to
the subject matter covered. It is sold with the understanding that neither the author nor the
publisher is engaged in rendering legal, investment, accounting, or other professional services.
While the publisher and author have used their best efforts in preparing this book, they make
no representations or warranties with respect to the accuracy or completeness of the contents
of this book and specifically disclaim any implied warranties of merchantability or fitness
for a particular purpose. No warranty may be created or extended by sales representatives or
written sales materials. The advice and strategies contained herein may not be suitable for
your situation. You should consult with a professional when appropriate. Neither the publisher
nor the author shall be liable for any loss of profit or any other commercial damages,
including but not limited to special, incidental, consequential, personal, or other damages.

Cover design and layout by: Streetlight Graphics, LLC

Paperback ISBN: 979-8-9912629-3-4
Hardcover ISBN: 979-8-9912629-4-1

Business Transitions Publishing, LLC
Lexington, KY
Printed in the United States of America

OTHER BOOKS BY DAVID GRAU SR., JD, AVAILABLE THROUGH AMAZON.COM:

Building With the End in Mind: A Complete Succession Planning Guide for Professional Service Owners

Succession Planning for Financial Advisors/Building an Enduring Business

Buying, Selling and Valuing Financial Practices

This book is dedicated to the future generations of professionals who have the opportunity to continue a tradition, a culture, and a business, all the while having the courage to change and improve on what they have acquired with no apologies.

Table of Contents

YOUR GUIDE 1

THE INTENDED AUDIENCE 5

THE BASIC PREMISE 9

NOTATE BENE 11

CHAPTER ONE: **OPPORTUNITIES & OBLIGATIONS**

SECTION 1: You Have Important Choices To Make 15

SECTION 2: Appreciating Your Earning Power 17

SECTION 3: Making A Living Vs. Building Wealth 18

SECTION 4: What Is A Succession Plan? 20

SECTION 5: How Exit Plans And Continuity Plans Differ 21

SECTION 6: What Exactly Are You Buying Into? 23

SECTION 7: Building An Equity-Centric Business 25

CHAPTER TWO: **THE COMPELLING MATH OF A SUCCESSION PLAN**

SECTION 1: The Three-Basket Cash Flow System 33

SECTION 2: Your Equity Blueprint 36

SECTION 3: Where Does The Money Come From? 40

SECTION 4: Bank Financing Vs. Seller Financing 43

SECTION 5: The Issue Of Basis **46**

SECTION 6: It's A Buy-In, Not A Buy-Out **48**

SECTION 7: Tax Efficiencies In A Succession Plan **50**

SECTION 8: Using Residual Equity To Your Advantage **53**

CHAPTER THREE: A TEAM BUILT FOR THE AGES

SECTION 1: What Does It Mean To Build A Legacy? **57**

SECTION 2: Developing A Successor Team **59**

SECTION 3: The Issue Of Tenure **62**

SECTION 4: Family Members On The Payroll **65**

SECTION 5: Assembling A Professional Support Team **67**

SECTION 6: No Book Builders Allowed **70**

CHAPTER FOUR: EXAMINING THE ESSENTIAL ENTITY FRAMEWORK

SECTION 1: Entity Structuring Basics **75**

SECTION 2: The Benefits Of A Limited
Liability Company **79**

SECTION 3: The Benefits Of An S-Corporation **82**

SECTION 4: Using A Hybrid Model **85**

SECTION 5: How Stock Is Bought, Sold, Or Redeemed **88**

SECTION 6: Granting And Gifting Stock **92**

CHAPTER FIVE: BUSINESS VALUE AND VALUATION

SECTION 1: Business Valuation Basics **99**

SECTION 2: Fair Market Value **103**

SECTION 3: Minority Discounts / Price Vs. Value **106**

SECTION 4: Rethinking Compensation From A
Valuation Perspective **109**

SECTION 5: Business Debt And Its Impact On Value **112**

SECTION 6: The Role Of Life Insurance **115**

CHAPTER SIX: **CONTROL MECHANISMS (OR, *HAVING A SAY IN THE PROCESS*)**

SECTION 1: The Levels Of Control 119

SECTION 2: The Roles And Responsibilities Of Officers 123

SECTION 3: Installing A Board Of Directors 126

SECTION 4: Voting And Non-Voting Stock 129

SECTION 5: Drag-Along Rights & Tag-Along Rights 130

SECTION 6: Shareholder And Director Meetings 132

CHAPTER SEVEN: LEARNING TO BE A GOOD BUSINESS PARTNER

SECTION 1: Being A Good Steward Of Ownership 137

SECTION 2: Overcoming G1's Objections 139

SECTION 3: What To Expect As A New Owner 144

SECTION 4: Family Members As Owners – Making It Work 147

SECTION 5: Taxes, Taxes, Taxes 150

SECTION 6: Helping G1 Let Go Gradually And Gracefully 153

SECTION 7: What If Your Succession Plan Fails (Or Trends In That Direction)? 155

CHAPTER EIGHT: THE IMPORTANCE OF BUSINESS GROWTH AND DEVELOPMENT

SECTION 1: Grow, Grow, Grow! 161

SECTION 2: Unlocking Growth   Scaling A Professional Services Business 166

SECTION 3: Putting The "M" Back In "M&A" 169

SECTION 4: Benchmarking (Against The Right Businesses) 171

SECTION 5: Working With A Coach And/Or Mentor 173

SECTION 6: Developing A Niche And A Specialty 175

CHAPTER NINE: **ARE YOU READY TO BE AN OWNER?**

    SECTION 1: Starting A Business Vs. Buying In 180

    SECTION 2: A Modern Day Apprenticeship 184

    SECTION 3: Dealing With Acquisition Debt 187

    SECTION 4: Is Synthetic Equity A Better Alternative? 189

    SECTION 5: Dealing With The Buy-In Documentation 192

    SECTION 6: Criteria For Ownership 194

    SECTION 7: When G1 Says "No" To Additional Owners 197

INDEX 205

ACQUIRING YOUR FUTURE THROUGH A SUCCESSION PLAN

DAVID GRAU SR., JD

YOUR GUIDE

As in the first book of this series, I put this section up front because I want you to know who your guide is and where the advice in this book comes from. This is a non-fiction book, after all, and it contains many details about buying and selling equity, financing the purchase, running and growing a business, building personal wealth, building business value, and more. If you are going to read such advice, let alone act on it, I think the background of your guide matters, a lot.

In short, I am a technician. I gravitate to the details of the succession planning process. I am an expert in legally and financially connecting the generations of ownership in a professional services business. It is what I know. It is what you can expect in the pages that follow. I do not do theory and fluff, and I don't offer lots of quotes from famous people to make you feel better about this quest, or about me. And while the mechanics of this process are consistent, whether you are a founder or a next gen buyer/investor, perspective changes everything. This book is written to guide younger buyers and investors who are considering this special type of ownership opportunity.

I can effectively author this book because I was in your same position at the start of my professional services career. I did what you may well do. I was a next generation owner who elected to buy out the senior partners in our professional services business. I took on a lot of personal debt and responsibility, worked an untold number of hours, improved on what I acquired, and never looked back. And I am here to tell you from experience that what I did is not for everyone. You may be the future, but you will have to earn it and pay for it. I will show you how, but I am not here to talk you into anything. I will present the opportunities and the obligations and trust you to make your own decision. But you do have a series of interesting and important decisions to make; we will start there in Chapter One.

I am schooled in the law, securities regulation, business taxation, entity design and structure, and business building. After several years of working as a Securities Regulator in the early 1990s, I opened my own securities law practice. In the beginning, I was a force of one, *hanging out my shingle* and figuring out how to run a practice from the ground up. But in truth, I owned a job that depended entirely on me to generate income, handle marketing, sales, and customer service. If we had a bad day, I could have a heart-to-heart talk with the owner every morning. And we had many such talks!

In time, I sold my law practice and used the money to start a professional services business specializing in succession planning, exit planning, and business valuation. Twenty-five years later, this business had grown from two people to sixty-five employees, a multi-million dollar annual payroll, a Marketing Team and a Sales Team, a full-time bookkeeping/accounting staff, and so on. In this small dynamic business, we *cracked the code* on succession planning and helped professional service owners design and implement the very plans addressed in this book. Along the way, we worked with many, many next generation professional service providers to help them understand the process and decide whether to become an owner or not.

And then I completed my own succession plan, selling my equity incrementally back to the business I started and to our own next generation owners, all of whom I hired directly or indirectly. This business then continued on without me, and that completed the circle...up to that point. I *kind of* retired and now am working on this, my fourth book. It won't be my last.

I have had three previous books published on this subject matter and I authored a monthly column in *Financial Planning Magazine* for six years on the subjects of succession planning, business perpetuation, and valuation. I have written and published dozens of professional white papers, have won a host of awards, graced a magazine cover or two, and been the subject of numerous articles for my contributions and thought leadership. I hope I can be of assistance to you in fulfilling your business dreams.

THE INTENDED AUDIENCE

Let's start with the age group for this book's intended audience—the whole point of a book written for next generation professionals. Experience dictates that about 90% of the next generation Professional Service Providers (PSPs) that this book is written for and will help are thirty-something years of age, with the other 10% scattered between the late twenty-something year olds and the early forty-something year olds. Statistically, that is the window of opportunity. I will often refer to the thirty-something-year-old group specifically in the following chapters, but understand that the term of art includes a slightly wider age range.

We generally call this group of thirty-something year olds, G2s for Generation Two; the next generation after that is called G3s and so on. It is the founders', or G1s', starting date that determines everything that follows, as does who will succeed them in ownership. Most generational gaps range from 12 to 15 years and are not a true generation of around 25 years. It is all about the math, as you will learn. And the working assumption is that today's G2s and tomorrow's G3s are not founders but are Professional Service Providers (PSPs) who aspire to ownership. I authored this book specifically to help you, G2 and G3, understand the process and the mechanics of becoming an owner.

For those thirty-something year olds who just started their own business and are already an owner, the applicable term is G1; it is not about your age or what your generation is called. To be clear, this is not a G1 or founder's book—that was the first book in this series, and that path differs significantly from yours, G2 and G3.

Moving on, the term **Professional Services**, at least for the succession planning strategies referred to in this book, includes any job, practice, or business (terms that we will define in Chapter One) whose core output is a service requiring specialized knowledge or skill and often requiring a professional degree, license, certification or registration. A key aspect of Professional Services is providing solutions to problems encountered by individuals and businesses. Examples of Professional Services include:

Acting Coaches/Workshops	IT Services/Computer Science
Accounting and Tax Practices	Legal Services/Law Firms
Advertising and Marketing Agencies	Logistics and Transportation
Analytics Services	Media & Entertainment
Architectural Firms	Payroll Services
Bookkeeping Services	Public Relations Firms
Business Valuation Firms	Publishing/Writing Services
Consulting Firms	Real Estate Brokerages
Contractors (Electrical, Mechanical, etc.)	Research & Development
Counselors	Software & Information Technology
Creative Agencies	Speech Pathologists
Dental Services	Storage Service Providers
Doctors and Medical Groups	Systems Integration Services
Engineering Services	Technology Consultants
Environmental Technology	Painters or Painting Companies
Event Management	Therapists
Financial Services/ Wealth Management	Travel, Tourism & Hospitality
HR/Benefit Firms	Web Developers and Designers
Independent Insurance Professionals	

...and the list goes on and on. These Professional Service owners and providers face unique challenges when it comes to perpetuating the work that they do and the services that they deliver, but they also have some distinct advantages as you will discover in our explorations.

The founders generally expect the successors in these succession plans to purchase ownership, or equity, at or about Fair Market Value, and invest their individual time and efforts and entire working careers in the process—these are long term, actively held investments. This aspect sets such plans and planning strategies apart from books and authors who write about organizational succession planning, as in trying to find the next CEO to lead a company. This book is about *ownership level* succession planning for privately held businesses. While we're at it, this is also not a book about your career track or management skills or how to get noticed. G2/G3, I am assuming that if you're reading this book, you are already very good at what you do and you want to learn how to take your work and your wealth building to the next level, that of being an owner, or an equity partner.

It should be apparent that with so many different types of Professional Services offered, there will be vast differences in how practices or businesses operate in terms of growth rates, overhead expenses, compensation, and profitability. There will be Professional Service businesses that generate 40% to 50% profitability, or EBITDA, while others will work just as hard and take all the commensurate risks to generate just 8% to 12% in profits. Regardless, a well-designed succession plan can work well at both ends of the performance spectrum.

I write what I know, and that factors into the intended audience as well. The succession plans I consulted on and helped to design during my career, to date, ranged from small practices with just one or two owners, often a parent and a son or daughter, to larger businesses with 20 owners from multiple generations. Valuations for these practices and businesses varied from $500,000 to more than $50 million, with the majority falling between $1,000,000 and $15,000,000. In the professional services world, this is my area of authority.

THE BASIC PREMISE

This book is about one generation helping another. But as a thirty-something year old **Professional Service Provider** (or **PSP**), you actually have several good choices in front of you. Time is on your side. Your choices include working as an employee or a contractor indefinitely, buying another PSP's practice and/or starting your own small business, or buying an equity interest in the business where you work or would like to work. This book delves into the concept of ownership, particularly exploring how the next generation of PSPs can invest in their workplace and become partners through a formal succession plan. I certainly won't and don't ignore your other choices, but the mechanical aspects of this *buy-in approach* are certainly given priority.

The process of building and operating a multiple-owner and multiple-generational business is called **Succession Planning**. As you will learn, most succession plans require at least two or more up-and-coming PSP's per business. This means that we (as in myself and all G1s) collectively need to help you, and many others like you, prepare and become educated on why you should seriously consider investing in the business where you work (or another similar business that makes you an offer) and not start your own. The Professional Services landscape is littered with one-generational books and practices that end with the founder's career; relatively few have any significant value and are sold. Your help and support are needed to move beyond this base model. The benefits of building on top of an existing business are many, and impact far more people than just the PSPs directly involved.

But don't think this is going to be easy or that the future is patiently waiting for you on your terms. So you are talented, ambitious, and you want more. Terrific. You need to genuinely want this, earn the chance, and then settle the opportunity by signing one or more personal promissory notes and servicing the debt for a period of up to ten to twenty years, and working even harder and smarter. "Opportunities and Obligations" was the alternative tag line for the title of this book and it is accurate. I thought you should hear this up front.

Regardless of the path you choose, I cannot help but think as I sit here writing this in my mid-60s, how much my career could have been positively impacted if I had the information in this book as a thirty-something year old lawyer and next gen PSP. I didn't know most of these strategies even existed.

Like most every PSP I've ever met, my goal with this book is to make a difference. Maybe we can do that together.

NOTATE BENE

1. You may notice that sometimes I use the terms "we" or "our" when providing my thoughts and guidance. I am the sole author of this book, but I worked alongside many talented, smart, dedicated professionals who helped to shape the strategies that I now write about. My use of these inclusive terms serves to honor my former teammates.

And this book is written to "you," the next generation Professional Service Provider, or PSP, and not to G1. We often will refer to you as "G2/G3" because it is not unusual for G1 to skip over or miss the G2 ownership level due to a late start, misperceptions, a lack of planning and such. One of the purposes of this book, G2, is to help you fix that problem!

2. I introduced the terms G1, G2, and G3 in my first succession planning book, written in 2013 for the financial services profession to denote each generation of ownership (see *Figure 1*). Though the terms have been widely accepted and adopted within the financial services world,

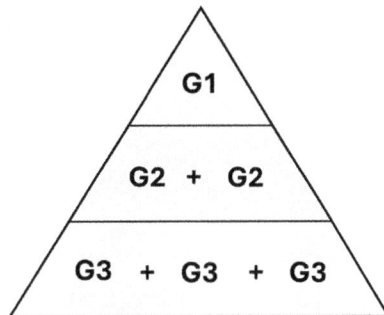

Figure 1

these will be new terms to the broader Professional Services space. G1s are the founders who start a business; G2s follow next, and G3s follow the G2s. In a succession plan between a parent and a son or daughter, the G1 and G2 labels are clear and concise, but in most cases, it is not that simple.

Most founders, or G1s, sell their equity to multiple next generation owners and at different times and intervals. Some G1s are younger, or the same age, as the G2s they hire and mentor; a participant's age really isn't the point. The G1/G2/G3 concept is great for teaching and learning the general sequence of the participants in a succession plan, and that's how we'll use the terms throughout this book. No matter what generation or age you are, there's a place for every smart, industrious, and creative team member. This book targets G2 and G3 level owners—the next generation of PSPs seeking future ownership to continue the G1-founded business. Hold on to that concept and we'll call it good.

3. Corporate terminology, including shares, shareholders, bylaws, and officers, will be used throughout this book to simplify the concepts and maintain a consistent voice. Limited Liability Companies, my personal preference, actually use different terms such as units of ownership, Members, and Managers, an Operating Agreement; for the most part, it doesn't matter. If there is a material difference from one entity structure to another other than terminology, I will tell you. Otherwise, I will focus on the concepts important to the succession planning process without getting mired down in the various entity structuring terms and nuances. In the end, your final set of documents should use the terms appropriate to the entity you choose, or the one that is already set up and you are considering investing in.

Similarly, references to owners receiving *compensation* for their work, *being on the payroll, receiving a paycheck,* or a *Guaranteed Payment to Partner (GPP)* are to be loosely applied because it depends on the entity structure or structures. There is an old saying that "owners get paid last" and it is an old saying that is still around for a reason. As an owner, and regardless of your age, generation, or amount of equity, there are no guarantees that you will be paid every two weeks or once a month. If the cash isn't in the bank, you and your fellow owners may come last on the list of a business's obligations. Welcome to learning to think like an owner!

4. Capitalized terms such as Professional Services, Professional Service Providers, Succession Planning, a Practice or a Business, etc., represent specifically defined terms in this book. The first defined use of such keywords is in bold type. You can then either look back to the end of each Chapter for the terms specifically defined therein, or to the Index at the end of this book. Succession planning has its own language, and this book will help you understand it and begin to speak it with authority.

5. Audiobooks and eBooks travel exceptionally well, and this book is published and available globally. While the strategies explored herein rely on the use of United States-based business entities, tax laws, and securities regulations, its core concepts should benefit any aspiring Professional Services owner. That said, regardless of your location, you will need to rely on local and professional legal/tax counsel before implementing any of the strategies in this book.

6. This is the second book in a two book series. The first book, *Building With the End in Mind: A Complete Succession Planning Guide for Professional Service Owners*, was published in late 2024 and is a detailed guide for the founders, perhaps your boss(s), or G1(s) as we'll call them. Both books in this series are or will be available as an eBook, paperback, hardbound, and audiobook, and are available through a wide variety of different distribution centers including Amazon, Barnes & Noble, Apple Books, Goodreads, Chirp, and many others.

G2, G3, if you are the one leading the succession planning initiative in your business, and that is not unusual, please buy your boss a copy *of the other book* and ask them to read it. You will then each know what you need to know from your unique perspectives, which should foster a great conversation about the future.

Thank you for buying this book and reading as much of it as you like. Can there be any more Important Note?!

And with that, let's get started. The future is right around the corner…

CHAPTER ONE: OPPORTUNITIES & OBLIGATIONS

(If you have not read the preceding introductory sections—*Your Guide, The Intended Audience, The Basic Premise, and Notate Bene* or, Important Notes—it would be a good idea to do so before proceeding through this and the following Chapters. Trust your guide.)

SECTION 1: YOU HAVE IMPORTANT CHOICES TO MAKE

As a next generation **Professional Services Provider**, or **PSP**, let's assume that you have chosen your profession and are busily honing your craft. You may be working as an intern, or an apprentice, probably as a W2 employee, or perhaps as an independent contractor. You may have chosen *to hang out your own shingle* right out of school which makes you a brave soul. More likely, you are selling your time or services at an agreed upon rate to an employer or business owner in exchange for the opportunity to learn, to observe, and to practice what you have chosen to do.

Of course, there is a financial element to these common, basic starting points. You need to make a living! In the background lie all the necessities and demands of life, as well as the rewards and the desired luxuries that tend to creep into the picture year after year as you climb the ladder of success. With student loans, perhaps a new house, a car, and such, generating income to pay off or service debt is also an important part of the picture. You may well be thinking to yourself as you read this paragraph, "Yes, and that is why I just need to keep working and earning money for the first ten to fifteen years or so of my professional life. Business ownership in the short term is out of the question."

Since you're reading this book, I am going to assume that you are open to new ways of thinking and exploring the opportunities in front of you. As I walked the same path and had the same thoughts, I will remind you that acquiring a 5% to 10% equity stake does not change your ability or need to keep working and making a living. The two concepts are actually complimentary in that ownership can provide you with *additional* streams of income and tax benefits that help you make a good living, actually a better living, and gradually build wealth at the same time. My argument is that you cannot afford NOT to look seriously into ownership and the sooner the better, even if that is not today.

In this first Chapter, I will lay out the foundational elements you need to understand and consider as you look forward to ownership opportunities in an existing Professional Services business:

- What are you investing in?

- How does equity, or stock, work and what do you actually own?

- Where does the money come from to service the debt when you buy in?

- What are the specific opportunities and obligations of such an investment?

- What are the tax benefits? What are the tax burdens?

- How does going into debt to buy equity in a professional services business help you build wealth?

We will start with these basics and build on them in subsequent Chapters, but let's add one more important question to the list—perhaps the most important question of all.

Will you own your future and acquire an equity interest in a business, or will you work for those who have chosen to own theirs? The first question to ask and answer is as simple as that. Will you be an owner, or a worker for the owners? You might well say, "Well, maybe in ten to fifteen years…" And in the blink of an eye, twenty years later, it feels like it is too late. Just be aware. Regardless, as you continue to read and to think, don't shy away from this one direct question because the answer changes everything.

SECTION 2: APPRECIATING YOUR EARNING POWER

This is not a long Section, and it doesn't need to be. As a PSP, you are a valuable commodity in a business sense over time. And time is your ally.

Think about it—what is the value of your earning power over the course of your career? For example, if you start out earning $50,000 a year, and those earnings grow at the rate of 5% per year for 40 years, you will earn just over $6,000,000! If you start out earning $75,000 a year, you will earn just over $9,000,000 in 40 years. And if you start out earning just $35,000 a year, you will still earn just over $4,200,000. And the business that employs you for much or all of that time will profit from those same earnings.

Let's rephrase the question. If you had $1.0 million dollars to invest today in any private business, to hold for the rest of your life, what business would it be? Perhaps the one where you now work and, with an equity interest, the one you can actually exert a significant amount of control over and help grow? Think about that because we're going to explore that possibility in depth. Is there a better, enduring, growing opportunity you'd prefer, let alone an opportunity that comes with a paycheck?!

Thinking like an investor, G2 and G3, would you choose a different location other than where you've chosen to live now? Would you choose a different profession other than the one you've chosen for yourself to date? A different business other than the one you have chosen to work at. Perhaps, but you get the point. This is a pretty good place to start, or a good point to jump off from to a better, similar place.

G2/G3, you can choose how to handle these basic investment fact patterns. Growth is one thing, taxes are another, but both factor into the equation. As an employee for life, you can take home all the earnings referenced above at ordinary income tax rates—the highest possible federal rates in the United States...or you can build wealth at lower, even much lower tax rates, and cut years, maybe a decade or more, off of the 40-year timetable. It is up to you if you get started sooner than later. If you're going to work and make a living anyway, why not be smart about it and have the opportunity to build more wealth in the process?

This is the language of equity. This is how you need to learn to think and to speak, and we're already at work on that issue. Keep reading.

SECTION 3: MAKING A LIVING VS. BUILDING WEALTH

As a PSP, there is nothing like feeling the satisfaction of providing great services to an appreciative client base. There is also nothing wrong with making a good living and building personal wealth in the process. This is not a choice you have to make. The two concepts actually can and should work in tandem on the business front if you are an owner.

Simply stated, participation in a profitable, growing business can provide more effective wealth-building resources than being an employee or being self-employed. In terms of tax efficiencies, cash flow predictability and resiliency, there really is no comparison between owning a business and owning one's job—we will define all of these terms for you shortly, so hang on. Here is the argument and the evidence, at least in part.

Your compensation as an employee is taxed as ordinary income, the highest tax rate in the Internal Revenue Code, and not even including any city, county, and/or state taxes. You do not have the full opportunity to write off business-related expenses. You are not entitled to a share of the business profits, and you don't share in the appreciating value of the business as it grows over time, even as you work to make that happen. You have little to no say in the operations, hiring, or direction of the business. That is the world of an employee and, for the most part, an independent contractor. This is how people, and PSPs, make a living, and many do this for their entire lives.

Let's begin to explore the world of business ownership and, perhaps, expose you to something new and almost magical. If and when you buy an **Equity Interest**, or stock in the business where you work, you might acquire, for example, 5,000 shares of stock from your boss (or bosses) in their S-Corporation (you'll learn all about entity structures in Chapter Four). With a total of 100,000 shares authorized and issued, this means you own a 5% Equity Interest. You're an owner! This also means that you are entitled to receive, as a matter of law, 5% of the business's profits (at a lower tax rate than ordinary income in most states), 5% of the business's stock appreciation as it grows effectively tax free until the shares are sold, access to the financial statements of the business and a vote, or at least a say, in the operations. You directly benefit by helping to grow the business in which you are an owner. Oh, and you still get paid for the work that you do.

The basic formula that describes these results from your perspective as a G2/G3 owner is that of **Shareholder Value**, and we will come back to this concept again and again because it really matters:

WAGES + PROFIT DISTRIBUTIONS + STOCK APPRECIATION

This is ownership level thinking. The idea is that you will use most, but not all, of your profit distributions to service the debt on the stock you bought as multiple owners help to grow the business revenues. We generally assume that your wages are already spoken for, so this new, slightly more tax efficient revenue stream is used to pay down the debt. As the business grows and the profit dollars increase, the debt servicing can accelerate even as the value of the stock you hold grows tax free–far more information and details yet to come. That shifts the basic formula to this:

WAGES + PROFIT DISTRIBUTIONS – DEBT SERVICE + STOCK APPRECIATION

And then you do it all again, buying in another 5%, 10%, or more, five to seven years later. That's life as a G2/G3 owner and investor in a nutshell. In a business that grows at just 7% a year, you can see your investment double several times over with the help and best efforts of all involved. This is the difference between making a living and building wealth (along with making a living).

So powerful is this opportunity that I strongly encourage you to raise the issue of ownership during your initial interview as you apply for a position as a PSP with a potential employer. And if you're interviewed by the sole owner of the business, and it has always been that way, I'd listen carefully to that person's plans for the business. If you're applying to work for a practice that will be sold to someone else or will just one day fade away, consider your options carefully. You have some good choices and decisions to make and you need to appreciate the value of your earning power and your contributions over time.

SECTION 4: WHAT IS A SUCCESSION PLAN?

A **Succession Plan** is best defined as a documented series of steps, or **Tranches**, designed to gradually transition ownership, leadership, and revenue production responsibilities internally to the next generation of owners, collectively referred to as a **Successor Team**. As a next generation ownership prospect, and just in case you skipped over the introductory material, we apply the term **G2** to you, which stands for Generation Two, as compared to the founding generation, or **G1**. Over the course of a Succession Plan, the Successor Team often includes two or more G2s and, eventually, two or more **G3s**. In a growing, sustainable business, the ownership base must grow wider and younger over time.

A Succession Plan is equity-based and requires the use of an entity structure. The goal is sustainability, and it is best accomplished through a Plan design and structural framework that carefully coordinates the changing roles of the founder(s) and the Successor Team members over many years. One of the major advantages of being a G2 or G3 owner is the ability to build on top of an existing, growing business—you don't have to start from scratch and figure out how to run a business for the first time.

Most Succession Plans include the founder's continuing assistance and presence in the day-to-day operations for 10 to 20 years or more after the Plan starts, though every Plan is different and can adapt to the fact pattern at issue. Succession planning is an ongoing process and not a singular event. To this end, a G2 or G3 owner may well purchase **Equity** (i.e., shares of stock) over several Tranches, spanning a decade or two.

Simply stated, the only way for a small practice to grow into a larger and stronger business is to attract, retain and propel next generation talent—to hire great people, support, and reward them, and then step aside as you (G2s and G3s in this story) gain experience and gradually fulfill your new collective roles as owners. The cumulative, incremental, long-term investments of next-generation PSPs, along with the goals and benefits of such planning, differentiate succession plans from all other transition plans.

To be clear, the members of a Successor Team for a relatively small, privately owned Professional Services business are almost always full-time employees of that business, and even licensed if your Professional Services are regulated. All of this makes the process, and the people who participate in it…very engaging!

SECTION 5: HOW EXIT PLANS AND CONTINUITY PLANS DIFFER

Compare and contrast a Succession Plan to an **Exit Plan**, the latter of which is a complete sale of a book, practice or business to either an external third-party buyer, or an internal buyer such as a key employee, or son or daughter. Regardless of who the buyer is, an Exit Plan is completed in one step. The entire business is bought or sold in one transaction. Typically, an Exit Plan is asset-based as compared to a Succession Plan, which is stock, or Equity-based.

An Exit Plan is one possible result that can occur when the founding generation does not set up an internal Succession Plan to perpetuate the practice. As a thirty-something year old next gen PSP, this is a possibility to consider. You may be able to buy the entire practice all at once when G1 is ready to retire. If the opportunity arises and the timing and price are right, it can make a lot of sense. Having consulted on or watched over thousands of Exit Plan transactions, successful external buyers are often two to three times the size and value of the seller; internal buyers, usually key employee(s) of the practice, can succeed as well but often require more financial support or consideration from the seller(s) to make it work. Exit Plans are usually an attempt by the founding owner(s) to maximize the value of the practice for sale.

In that an Exit Plan transfers depreciable assets, rather than Equity or stock which are purchased on an after-tax basis, it can provide significant legal and tax benefits to the buyer (as compared to buying stock) that often positively, and perhaps significantly, affect the value paid to the seller. However, when an Exit Plan has been completed and the new owner takes over, the acquired book or practice is effectively absorbed into the buyer's business. From a seller's perspective, their book or practice ceases to exist; such a buyer, for this reason, is not a successor in a technical or legal sense.

A **Continuity Plan** is a written agreement that provides for an orderly transfer of ownership, control and responsibility in the event one of the owners of a business entity suddenly leaves, whether by choice or through a partnership dispute, a loss of licensure, death, or disability. In the case of a Succession Plan, with a G1 and a G2 owner, the two owners will serve as each other's continuity partners in a formal Continuity Plan. In this manner, a Continuity Plan serves a completely different purpose than an Exit Plan or a Succession Plan.

A Continuity Plan can also look to others outside of the business when there is a single owner or when the second owner in the business does not want to take on the obligation of buying out their partner on sudden notice. Solving for these issues becomes increasingly important, even critical, as the G1 ownership level grows older and their Equity Interest becomes increasingly valuable. This is a common reason G1 owners look to build a multi-generational ownership structure.

These professionally drafted Plans must anticipate a variety of triggering events and establish rules that determine who can buy the Equity and how it will be valued and paid for. Continuity Plans, depending on the entity structure, are also known as a **Shareholders' Agreement** (as with a corporation), a **Buy-Sell Agreement**, or an Operating Agreement that includes buy-sell provisions (for an LLC) or an LLC with a separate **Members Agreement**. As a G2 or G3 next gen PSP who owns an Equity Interest, you may be obligated to step up on a moment's notice and, along with any and all other Successor Team members, buy out a disabled or deceased or suddenly retiring or withdrawing G1 owner. A Continuity Plan is therefore both an *opportunity* to acquire more Equity and an *obligation* to pay for it.

The take away here is that a business should actually consider having a Succession Plan, a Continuity Plan, and as a back-up, an Exit Plan. It is not one or the other—it might well be all three. Smart business owners should have a full range of options at all times. G2/G3, you still need to know where you might fit into all of these different plans.

SECTION 6: WHAT EXACTLY ARE YOU BUYING INTO?

Asked in a different way, "What Exactly has G1 Built?" Not all foundations are equal, or equally strong. As a next generation Professional Services Provider, it is important that you understand what it is that you're contemplating investing in and building on top of. After all, you are effectively an active investor making a career-length investment into an intangible asset-based operation. The structure of the opportunity, be it a book, practice or business, will greatly impact your opportunities and obligations. From this point on, each of these terms is used specifically and not generically or interchangeably.

Respectfully, many PSPs have not built and do not own a Business; they own the Job that they do, or a Practice perhaps, but not a real

Business as we'll specifically define the term below. It makes a big difference to a buyer or investor. As we lay out the specifics of each of these models, it should become clear that owning a Job, or a Book of clients, or even a single-owner Practice, means owning a one-generational ownership model. The whole point of implementing a Succession Plan is to change and improve on this shortcoming.

We will use the synonymous terms of owning one's **Job** or owning a **Book** of clients or customer relationships to describe the base model ownership structure in the Professional Services world. A Book is best described as a single individual, often a sole proprietor, who may work from an executive suite or from home, and sometimes on a revenue-sharing basis under someone else's office lease. A Book owner, in almost all cases, has not made a significant investment in an operational structure of their own. Simply stated, the purpose of this ownership model is to generate revenue—find clients and earn a living. At career end, professionals may sell their assets (a client list, cash flow, goodwill), but typically their career and client base just fade away, and they refer any remaining clients to other professionals. For the sake of simplicity, we will just use the term Book when referring to this level of ownership.

By the way, lest I appear dismissive of owning and building a Book, the most common ownership structure and the starting place for so many Professional Service owners and providers, think again. Individually, Book owners can play a special role in the Succession Planning process by effectively merging into a larger, more lucrative Business, tax free in most cases if the Business entity structure is set up properly in advance. We will address this unique and powerful tool set in Chapter Four. So to those of you who might be Book owners, understand that your path may well be destined to cross with a Business owner and that might be a very good thing for both of you.

The term **Practice** refers to a level of ownership that is larger and stronger than a Book. Practice owners tend to have a formal entity structure, commonly an LLC or a corporation, electing to be taxed as an S-Corporation. Practices, by our definition, have just one owner or shareholder. An owner of a Practice invests in office space through a formal lease agreement, has at least a small support staff and has the basic infrastructure (desks, computers, furniture, fixtures, etc.) to support growth, often including a Line of Credit and/or business credit or charge cards. Practices can be quite valuable with some in the $1,000,000 to $5,000,000 range, and may attract or operate alongside other Book owners in a coordinated fashion. A Practice is not limited to being a one-generational model—with time and a good plan, a Practice can grow into a full-fledged Business capable of supporting a long-term Succession Plan.

A **Business** is best defined for our purposes as an enterprise that is not only larger and stronger than a Practice, it is more sophisticated. A Business uses a professional compensation system (for employees and owners) that supports a strong *bottom line* on the Profit & Loss Statement. Profitability is one of the keys to differentiating this level from the preceding two levels of ownership. Profit distributions, in turn, are used to augment the compensation system for Equity owners and to recruit, retain, and reward next generation PSPs who invest in Equity and are part of an internal Successor Team Sustainability is another key here, and it is, or is destined to become part of the culture, supported by a Succession Plan and a Continuity Plan among the Equity partners. New hires (future G2s and G3s) to this level of ownership should fully anticipate having the opportunity to work hard/smart and, one day, to buy in and become an owner or equity partner of the Business.

Commit these terms to memory, as you'll read them many times in the pages to come, but always within the context of these definitions. Books, Practices, and Businesses represent different opportunities for you, and perhaps, different obligations and challenges as an investor—understand the difference.

SECTION 7: BUILDING AN EQUITY-CENTRIC BUSINESS

The most valuable asset that most G1 level PSPs own is their Practice or their Business. Between the cash flow it provides, the tax benefits, and the appreciating Equity value over time, there often is no close second-place finisher in this category. A Succession Plan empowers you, as a G2 or G3 level owner, to buy in and make it work in the same way over the course of your career.

The starting point is to figure out what you have the opportunity to invest in. A Professional Services Practice, if it is to grow into a Business, must move away from revolving around one person's talent, drive, and personality, often that of the founder. This *force of one* approach (individually or by generation) is a common trait of a Book or Practice model; it does not work at the Business level. This seismic shift in thinking is a big part of building an **Equity-Centric** Business, as opposed, perhaps, to an ego-centric business.

The term *Equity-Centric* refers to prioritizing Equity as the basis for value and the measurement of success, rather than focusing primarily on client relationships and revenue production. A Succession Plan is built upon an Equity-Centric business model. The five attributes of an Equity-Centric Business are these:

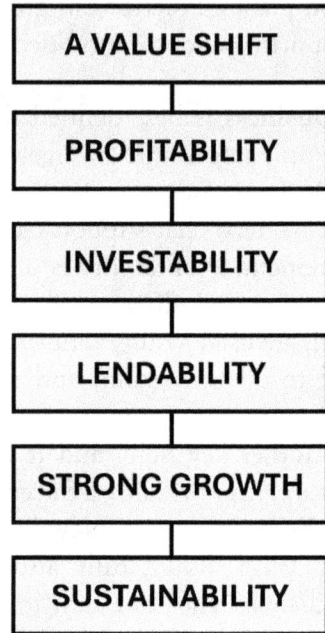

| A VALUE SHIFT |
| PROFITABILITY |
| INVESTABILITY |
| LENDABILITY |
| STRONG GROWTH |
| SUSTAINABILITY |

Figure 2

1. <u>A shift in value</u> from one or more individual producers to Equity in an entity structure

2. <u>A focus on profitability</u> as the measure of value and success

3. The building of an <u>investable business</u>

4. A business capable of <u>consistent top-line growth</u> year-over-year

5. A multi-generational, multi-owner business that achieves <u>sustainability</u> from one generation to the next

As the succession planning process itself evolves in the wider universe of Professional Services, if I could add one more attribute for the future, it would be that the Business opportunity <u>is lendable</u> (see *Figure 2*). Investors, or next generation PSPs, will require support from a capable money source to acquire an Equity Interest. A reliable banking partner plays a crucial role in this process. And keep in mind that sellers are more likely to be open to selling a significant stake in their Business at Fair Market Value when they receive a check, in full, in return.

Thinking this out, you cannot be a part of or invest in a Succession Plan without at least some of these foundational elements already in place, with the rest coming later. A G1 owner could, however, set up a business with all of these elements and still see the Succession Plan fail or fall short and decide instead on an Exit Plan. Yet another possibility includes forced or contractual reliance on the terms of a Continuity Plan to bring matters to an end, or a turning point. The takeaway here is that people can't work forever; a well-structured Business can indeed outlive its owners. As a part of this Chapter, let's explore just the first attribute of what it means to be Equity-Centric, a shift in the value proposition. We'll cover each of the other attributes in greater detail in the Chapters that follow.

Most Professional Service owners begin as *forces of one*, and if not as an actual sole proprietorship, then a single owner S-Corporation or LLC; sometimes it is a small group of similarly aged PSPs. At some point early in the process, all owners need a single entity structure to build around. For the duration of this book, we'll refer to the preferred entity structure as **Newco, LLC**, or **Newco** since a Limited Liability Company can basically adapt any cash flow or tax structure, upon election, that the founding owner(s) desires.

Establishing or amending the proper entity structure to support a Succession Plan is the first step. The second step is that the assets of the individual founder(s) or PSPs are literally and legally transferred into Newco, the entity. Pause for a moment, please, and just focus on this and the next couple of paragraphs. Hold on to these concepts as we work through them. This is what you need to know…the assets of a Professional Services sole proprietorship are basically these, regardless of the profession one is engaged in:

(a) The clients (or client list) being served

(b) The annualized cash flow generated from serving the clients

(c) Any tangible property (the physical tools of the trade or profession, whatever they may be), and

(d) Goodwill

Collectively, we refer to these as **Capital Assets**. This is the part that most Professional Service owners overlook, or fail to understand, to their peril. It is the first if not primary reason a Practice never becomes a sustainable and investable Business and dies at the end of its founder's career.

Using a legal contract, all rights, title and interest in the Capital Assets of the individual and founding PSPs must be transferred into Newco in exchange for a proportional amount of Equity. Newco, as a result of this formal exchange process, then becomes the legal owner of those valuable Capital Assets, including all future related revenue. The contributor or founding PSPs each become a shareholder of Newco (see *Figure 3*). All of this typically happens privately, quietly, and without any kind of government oversight (state or federal) when setting up a new LLC, and/or having it file an appropriate tax election. At this stage of the initial process, the transformation from a Book to a Practice to a Business formally begins. That is a lot to take in.

More simply, consider Newco's decision to be taxed as an S-Corporation upon setup with 1,000,000 authorized voting shares in a single class. The lone contributing and founding owner in this example, Bob, moves from individual or sole proprietor to shareholder with his conveyance of all of his Capital Assets to Newco. Now, Bob owns 1,000,000 authorized and issued shares of voting stock <u>and Newco owns all the Capital Assets</u>.

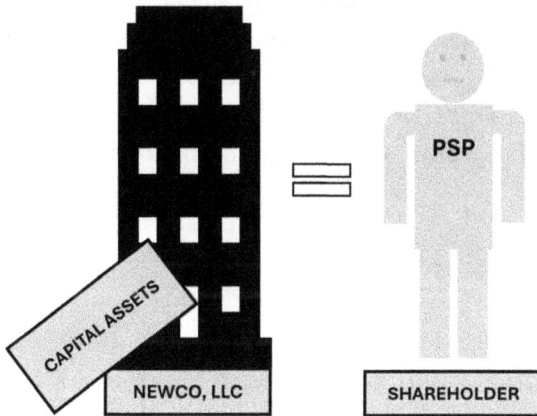

Figure 3

Here is why this matters. An appraiser can now value, or appraise, the Capital Assets that Newco legally holds and effectively determine a price per share–the Business has value. If the Business is valued at $2,500,000, for example, then each share of stock that Bob owns is objectively worth $2.50/share. Bob is then able to sell some of these shares to you, G2/G3, and you can choose to invest in these appraised shares and, possibly, obtain a bank loan to support your Equity purchase. This is the first step in building a Business that is more than a *force of one.*

It is also possible, even likely in a Professional Services model, that several affiliated individuals or Book owners could simultaneously make such contributions into Newco upon its set-up, effectively resulting in a merger of those individual Books via a series of tax-neutral exchanges. Newco might begin operations with two, three or four partners at one time. In such a case, Newco now owns ALL the contributed Capital Assets with each contributor owning Equity, proportionally. In most cases, this exchange process can be accomplished with no cash payments or any immediate tax consequences to the participants, if the rules are followed carefully and completely. This is actually a common method of forming a new Business with multiple contributing PSP owners. More details on this opportunity will be provided In the Chapters that follow.

The point is not to impress upon you that these maneuvers are easy. They are not. But these are common building blocks in the world of succession planning for PSPs and you need to understand how the basic mechanics work to even ask the right questions of your legal and tax counsel. If you know enough to ask, an answer can usually be figured out.

Lessons To Be Learned

- There is a vast difference between making a living and building wealth; partaking in a Succession Plan provides the opportunity to do both.

- A Succession Plan is a gradual ownership transition. An Exit Plan is a complete sale of a Practice or Business, all at one time. A Continuity Plan is a contractual agreement between two or more owners obligating each to step in and take over in the event one owner is disabled or deceased or needs to quickly retire.

- An Equity-Centric Business describes the foundation needed to support a Succession Plan. The attributes of such a Business include a shift in value from individuals to equity, plus profitability, investability, and consistent and strong top-line growth, all resulting in sustainability of the enterprise.

- There are significant differences between investing in a Book, a Practice, or a Business. As a prospective next generation PSP looking to invest your career into the place where you work, you need to know what the opportunity presents and what it may be capable of with your help.

- This book isn't about building larger, more complex businesses—it is about building stronger, longer-lasting businesses powered by the combined skills and thinking of multiple generations of ownership.

- G2/G3, you have choices to make.

Defined Terms in the Order Presented in this Chapter

- Professional Service Provider (or PSP)
- Equity Interest or Equity
- Shareholder Value
- Succession Plan
- Tranche(s)
- Successor Team
- G1/G2/G3
- Exit Plan
- Continuity Plan
- Shareholders Agreement
- Buy-Sell Agreement
- Members Agreement
- Job/Book
- Practice
- Business
- Equity-Centric Business
- Newco, LLC (or Newco)
- Capital Assets (contribution of…)

CHAPTER TWO:
THE COMPELLING MATH
OF A SUCCESSION PLAN

I heard it said somewhere along the way that there are three kinds of people in the world—those who are good at math and those who aren't. I'm an English major.

In the process of working with many thirty-something year old key employees, I've learned one thing for certain. Hours of good arguments and sound, logical reasoning as to why someone should, or should not, become an owner, cannot compare to a single, detailed, pro forma spreadsheet laying out the plan. The numbers tell their own story; like the blueprints of a building.

SECTION 1: THE THREE-BASKET CASH FLOW SYSTEM

Once Newco, LLC is properly set up, or the existing entity is rebuilt to support a Succession Plan, a business bank account can be opened. Granted that, as a G2/G3 ownership prospect, these tasks will probably already be done by G1, but let's proceed with the basic concepts for learning purposes. From this moment onward, with all Capital Assets having been properly and legally transferred into the entity, all incoming revenue generated by Newco and its owner(s) and producers, or PSPs, will be deposited into Newco's primary checking account. In turn, this revenue will create the first lines of Newco's Profit & Loss Statement, or P&L.

This income should then be *compartmentalized* as it flows through the P&L to more clearly illustrate the concept of profitability as needed to support a Succession Plan through the underlying Equity-Centric Business. This Section is about cash flow management and rethinking the process from an owners' perspective.

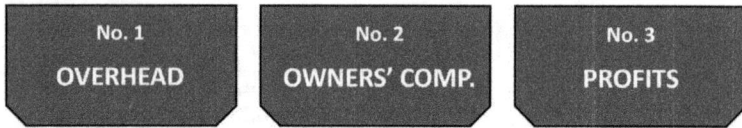

No. 1	No. 2	No. 3
OVERHEAD	OWNERS' COMP.	PROFITS

Figure 4

Start with the notion that all incoming revenue from all owners and PSPs flows into three different "baskets" in Newco's Equity-Centric cash flow system. The first basket (picture a large, hand-woven, wicker, laundry-sized basket if you will!) is set aside for general overhead expenses, the second basket is reserved for owners' compensation, and the third basket is what is left over, or profits, literally the bottom-line of Newco's rebuilt P&L (see *Figure 4*).

The general idea is this—overhead, Basket No. 1, is the cost of running the business and encompasses all expenses except for owner salaries. Basket No. 2 is for the owner(s) total annual base salary/salaries, or more accurately, wages for the work they perform. These two baskets serve to acknowledge that everyone, including and especially the owner(s), must be paid for the work that they do. These two baskets also provide notice that not every dollar of revenue after overhead expenses from Basket No. 1 have been paid is allocated to the owner's salary as it would be in a sole proprietorship (the training grounds for most entrepreneurs).

In fact, there are often tax advantages to be gained by isolating and limiting the amount of money paid through Basket No. 2, in deference to Basket No. 3. In the end, it is Basket No. 3, profits or profitability, which is the measure of success and the primary determinate of Business value. To an investor (a term used broadly to include all owners of the Business), Basket No. 3 provides the return on each owners' investment (or **ROI**). Every small business and Professional Services venue is unique but let's start out with a guideline of 25% profitability as a reasonable, near-term future goal and adjust from there, acknowledging that some Professional Services can only generate half that, and others, twice that. This strategy and logic still apply regardless of what *normal* profitability is for your specific Professional Services model.

If Newco, for example, generates $1,000,000/year in gross revenue for services rendered, then after Basket Nos. 1 and 2 are satisfied, $250,000 flows to the bottom-line of Newco's P&L and flows home, pro rata, to the owner(s) of this tax conduit or flow through entity structure (terms explained in more depth in Chapter Four). Basket No. 3, along with compensation for work performed from Basket No. 2, is a large part of what creates and supports the concept of a Business being investable for the Successor Team members. But to be clear, the only way to access the dollars in Basket No. 3, often in a more tax efficient manner as compared to Basket No. 2, is to take the risk of ownership and acquire an Equity Interest.

One of the primary goals of using this **Three-Basket Cash Flow System** is to help newer, younger owners learn to *think and act like an owner*. Creating a successful enterprise necessitates constant monitoring of general business expenses. Given that the next generation owners who buy Equity will need to use much of their future profit distribution checks from Basket No. 3 to pay for their investment, growing the top-line of the Business while limiting the amount of overhead and owners' compensation, within reason, leads to greater value and a shorter debt service period. Effectively, the Successor Team members are motivated to use "smart and efficient growth" to build value and to address their debt service obligations. This Three-Basket Cash Flow System is often detailed in the pro forma spreadsheet models with cash flow projections tracked annually.

For those Professional Service owners whose venue requires much higher overhead that, in turn, reduces profitability to the 10% to 15%

range, please keep reading. Doctors, dentists, veterinarians, lawyers, just to list a few such learned professionals, are expensive to hire and retain, but the lessons on how to balance cash flows more effectively and how to use Equity to hold expenses and salaries down in favor of more tax efficient rewards (stock appreciation and profit distributions) are still very much worth considering. At the very least, bolstering profitability by even a couple percentage points over your competitors could change the value of a Business significantly whether it is built for Succession or is to be sold as part of an Exit Plan.

Every Business ownership team must find what works best for their Professional Services model and its geographical setting (which impacts the cost of doing business). The answers as to the proper cash flow system for any given Business often come from the pro forma spreadsheet modeling process. Of course, anything and everything works in this system where there is just one owner; modeling for two or three owners is a revelation.

SECTION 2: YOUR EQUITY BLUEPRINT

Nothing will be more informative to you as a G2/G3 investor than a forward-looking spreadsheet model that paints a detailed, yet conservative picture of the plan. Think of the spreadsheeting process, upon finalization, as your **Equity Blueprint**; this is the math that lays out the actual Succession Plan. With that in mind, let's start to work through some of the numbers you will need to better understand.

G2, your options as a participant in a Succession Plan depend on G1's start date and their anticipated retirement date, which may or may not be a hard stop or a complete retirement. Assume that G1's minimum time commitment in a formal Succession Plan is about ten years. A ten-year commitment by G1 often results in a 15 to 20 year commitment by the G2 buyers of G1's Equity due to the financing and overlapping amortization schedules. That's the first step in understanding the math—you can buy a lot more house with a twenty-year mortgage than a ten-year mortgage. Here is an example to better explain this important concept.

Tranche One (T1) can be used to shift 200,000 shares of G1's 1,000,000 shares of stock in Newco to two G2s whom we'll call G2(A) and G2(B). Each next gen PSP buys 100,000 shares from G1 on the same date and at the same price per share. (We tend to recommend one-million shares because it keeps the price per share down to single or double digits even in a fast growing Business.) This moves ownership from 100% G1 to an 80%/10%/10% ownership structure, G1/G2(A)/G2(B) respectively (see Figure 5). G1 collects two checks based on the Business's **Fair Market Value (FMV)** (defined in Chapter Five) at that moment in time, presumably at long-term capital gains tax rates and G2(A) and G2(B) each sign ten-year term notes with a local bank for conventional loans at the then applicable interest rate.

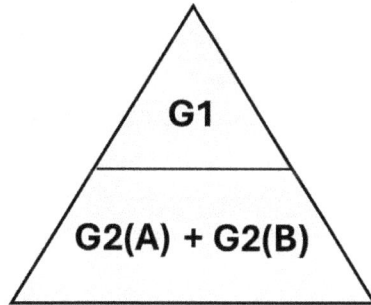

Figure 5

Four or five years later, if all is going well, **Tranche Two, or T2** is executed. The Business is reappraised at current FMV and G1 sells another 200,000 shares at FMV cumulatively to G2(A) and G2(B), moving ownership from 80%/10%/10%, to 60%/20%/20%, G1/G2(A)/G2(B) respectively. G1 receives two more checks from these sales (this is **Equity Income** to G1), and each Successor Team member signs another ten-year promissory note. The T2 loans for G2(A) and G2(B) will probably *overlap* their T1 loans which, ideally, should be paid off in about seven to eight years depending on current and anticipated growth rates and profitability levels. Each note and each financing process stands on its own in terms of cash flow to service the debt. This means that, in T2 for example, 10% of G2(A)'s profit distribution dollars will be modeled and used to specifically target the costs of acquiring 100,000 shares of stock in the second Tranche. The same strategy is applied in T1.

In terms of financing arrangements, when an individual purchases an

Equity Interest in a Business, they may pay the purchase price with cash on hand, with proceeds from a bank loan, and/or with seller financed debt. If a seller agrees to accept and personally hold a promissory note from a buyer for some or all of the purchase price (i.e., **Seller Financing**), the note payments may be structured in any number of ways. The two most common structures in succession planning purchases are fixed payment notes and profit-based notes. Under both of these payment structures, the purchase price for the Equity Interest is agreed upon and established at the time of sale. Shares of stock have a *strike price* on the day they are sold, even in a privately held Business. The price is often tied to the FMV of that Business as determined by an appraiser; the price per share does not change for those shares after the sale regardless of future business performance. Accordingly, earn-out arrangements which result in a variable purchase price are inappropriate as a payment device for an Equity purchase/sale.

With a fixed payment note, a buyer makes equal installment payments to the seller, with interest, over a set period, or term, in payment of a sum certain. A **Profit-Based Note**, on the other hand, allows each payment to vary because it is equal to a certain percentage (as defined in the Note) of each quarterly gross profit distribution the buyer receives from the Business during the term (see *Figure 6*). A Profit-Based Promissory Note must have a defined term, and if there is an outstanding balance on the Note at the end of the term, the buyer will be required to make a final lump sum payment to the seller, unless the seller agrees to extend the Note. A Profit-Based Note is also a promise to pay a sum certain. This Note structure is a strong motivator for all the owners to work together to grow the Business and to generate a high level of profitability for the duration of the Note.

Even for G2 owners who obtain a conventional bank loan, it still can make sense to develop an Equity Blueprint (spreadsheet model) that uses a Profit-Based Note format. Most banks do not offer this repayment method, but this is still an effective way to think through the math especially when the successive Tranches are expected to overlap each other (i.e., when a second Tranche begins before the first Tranche has been fully paid off, and so on). This makes overlapping Tranches cash flow more easily. Tranches do not have to overlap but they commonly do as a result of time constraints and an increasing share price which causes G2/G3 buyers to want to acquire additional Equity sooner.

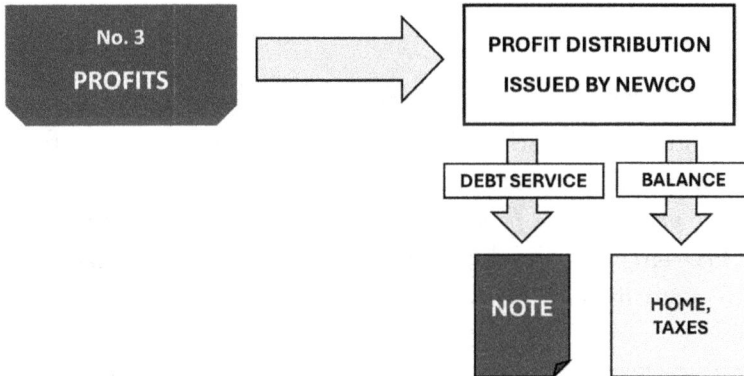

Figure 6

A good starting point, again for modeling purposes only, is to use only G2(A)'s after-tax profit dollars to service the debt from a purchase of Equity, assuming that G2(A)'s wage/compensation dollars are already spoken for. We try to limit the profit-based debt service to 70% to 85% of the available, after-tax profit distribution dollars in order to see the Note paid off in seven to eight years–of course, this depends on a host of other considerations such as FMV, actual sales price, growth rates, down payment, profitability and more. A *cushion* is or should be purposefully built in, just in case, and G2(A) is made aware that they can always devote more or all of their profit distribution dollars to service the debt and even some of their wages or savings if they so choose.

As each Tranche is paid for, servicing the debt for each succeeding Tranche tends to become easier and the amortization process tends to become shorter, or condensed, even as the price of Equity in a growing Business increases. In effect, there is an acceleration curve over the course of several Tranches. As an example, consider that when G2(A) finishes paying off T1 and now has 20% of the profit dollars available to them, they can use all or most of those dollars to finish paying off the 10% equity purchase in T2. The Profit-Based Note approach isolates each purchase for modeling and planning purposes because of the tendency to overlap the Equity buy-ins, but nothing stops G2(A) from further accelerating the process and retiring their debt sooner if the cash flow is there.

SECTION 3: WHERE DOES THE MONEY COME FROM?

The second characteristic of an Equity-Centric Business is a focus on profitability (Chapter One, Section 7). In sum, G2/G3 readers, this is *where the money comes from* to service the debt when you buy Equity from G1—high(er) levels of profitability fueled by steady, strong growth over time (see *Figure 7*).

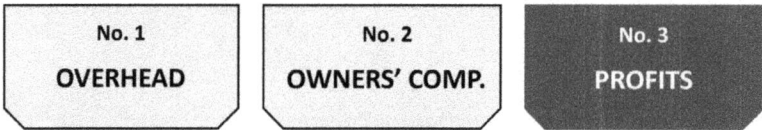

No. 1	No. 2	No. 3
OVERHEAD	**OWNERS' COMP.**	**PROFITS**

Figure 7

This money trail flows into and through a Business and can support either bank financing or Seller Financing which is covered in the very next Section.

From an appraiser's point of view, the bottom-line of a Business's Profit & Loss Statement, profitability, is the starting point for determining value. Annual gross revenue is often the primary measurement tool for success relied on by sole proprietorships including most Book and Practice owners, while profits are the primary measurement tool for Business owners. Profits, or what's left after all expenses and at least reasonable compensation to the owner(s) has been paid, is what investors are interested in because profits support growing share value. Profits are also one of the key factors that a next generation (G2 and/or G3) investor's bank looks to when considering a conventional or SBA loan to support such an investment—this is the developing attribute of being lendable.

Basket No. 3 is obviously important, but smart owners, G1 and G2/ G3 alike, will find that they have to focus as a team on carefully managing Basket Nos. 1 and 2 to achieve sufficient and appropriate levels of profitability. Overhead expenses, to a large degree, are the most difficult category to significantly reduce or change, though such expenses certainly warrant a firm grasp at all times. Most Practices, as they make the turn towards becoming a Business, start with lower profitability as compared to what they'll have in years to come or what a well-run competitor Business might have. A lower profitability picture might initially appear as 50%/40%/10%, applying our Three-Basket Cash Flow System. G2/G3, these **Performance Ratios** (annualized levels of overhead vs. owners' comp. vs. profitability) might be the picture you see when first invited to consider ownership. Initially, the math may not be all that compelling. This Section is about fixing the problem.

Again, I'll concede that almost everything works as to Basket No. 2 with an ownership team limited to the founder or founders since their base wages are augmented by the profits flowing through Basket No. 3, at least in the tax conduit models utilized throughout this book. The G1 ownership level can simply decrease the amount of cash in Basket No. 2 and effectively increase the amount of cash in Basket No. 3 within reason as it all flows through to the owners pro rata, anyway. With one G1 owner, or two or three equal G1 owners, it makes no difference.

The challenge and the opportunity to meaningfully adjust a Business's cash flow model for long-term success and profitability often comes when new, next generation investors join the ownership team. The impetus for change starts in an unlikely place, however, and that is Basket No. 2 (see *Figure 8*).

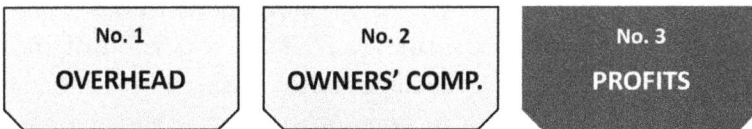

No. 1	No. 2	No. 3
OVERHEAD	**OWNERS' COMP.**	**PROFITS**

Figure 8

A simple guideline rule to understand is that new owners won't buy Equity, shoulder a ten-year amortization schedule, *and take a pay cut*. Whatever wages G2/G3 enjoyed recently as employees or Book owners, perhaps including part or all of a consistently earned annual bonus, will often translate into G2/G3's new wages as an owner (within reason). As such, G2/G3, your entrance into the Business tends to reset all the cash flow numbers. But the goal here is to reset those numbers in such a way as to maximize profitability as quickly as possible, with no one taking much if any kind of pay cut.

Consider what happens when G2(A), *a key employee* of the Business in this case, acquires Equity from G1. As a new owner, G2(A) stops being an expense (no disrespect intended) and those dollars now shift over to Basket No. 2 with the other G1(s). All wages for work performed by all the owners come out of this second, controllable cash flow Basket. A common strategy at this point is to consider that Basket No. 2 wages do not need to change or increase every year there-after. G2/G3, you will quickly learn that owners have more ways, and better ways, of being paid and building wealth than just wages plus a bonus all at ordinary income tax rates.

Let's begin by stabilizing Basket No. 2 wages <u>for all owners</u> once Tranche One has begun, using what we often call a **Plateau Level Compensation Strategy** (see *Figure 9*). Effectively, we freeze owners' compensation for three or four years at a time. The reason that you might consider this approach and freeze all the owners' compensation levels (owners can and should be paid different salaries based on their tenure, roles, and other factors) is because of the combined effects of profit distributions in a growing, efficient Business.

As a Business continues to grow on the shoulders of more owners, with everyone watching general overhead in Basket No. 1, and with Basket No. 2 stabilized, where do the new growth dollars go? Into Basket No. 3, of course. In the years ahead, a portion of the new growth dollars will have to be allocated to Basket No. 1, but not all of them. By directing little to none of the new growth monies into Basket No. 2, profitability will improve as a Business grows and much of the new money flows to the bottom-line of the P&L. Every three to four years, reset ownership compensation as a group and then stay at that new plateau level for a similar period.

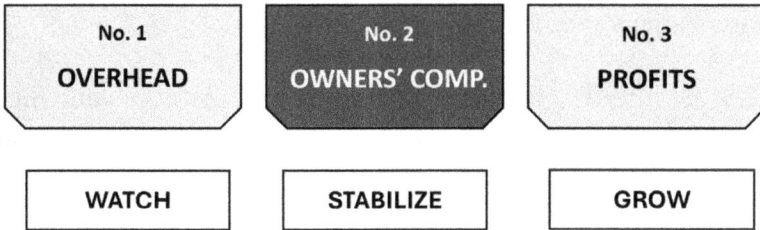

No. 1	No. 2	No. 3
OVERHEAD	**OWNERS' COMP.**	**PROFITS**
WATCH	**STABILIZE**	**GROW**

Figure 9

And now that I have your attention with that draconian compensation approach, G2 and G3, yes, it is OK to continue to receive some variable compensation including a (smaller) bonus and a **COLA** or **Cost of Living Adjustment**, within reason. Younger, next gen owners are always more sensitive to adjustments to their wages because they take home less of the profits than G1 and much of those profits are spoken for in terms of debt service. Wages, even at higher tax rates, are simply how money gets home for newer owners so this Plateau Level Compensation Strategy should be applied in a flexible manner to make it fit the circumstances.

The most common Performance Ratios to work towards in the first three to five years of setting up an Equity-Centric Business and adding new, next gen owners is something in the range of 40%/30%/30% (overhead/owners' comp/profits). A longer term cash flow model of 35%/30%/35% or 30%/30%/40% changes everything from an investor's point of view, depending of course on your Professional Services venue and normal, competitive overhead levels.

SECTION 4: BANK FINANCING VS. SELLER FINANCING

Not that long ago, Seller Financing was the norm in the Professional Services space for all Succession Planning transactions as well as most Exit Plans. In its simplest form, Seller Financing, sometimes called owner financing, is when the seller (or G1 in our case) acts as the lender in place of a traditional bank. A common phrase used to describe seller financing is that the seller "holds the paper," often in the form of a promissory note. *In the old days*, we said that "With seller financing, everything works!" And it did, and it still does, but it demands a patient and risk-tolerant seller.

G2/G3, let's begin with some context as you consider your financing alternatives. Over the past decade or two, banks began to change very gradually on this front. Banks started to consistently offer SBA, or Small Business Administration backed loans, for financial professionals, accounting firms, veterinarians, dentists, medical practices and such. This SBA-backed loan approach made sense because, from a lender's perspective, there aren't sufficient hard assets in most Professional Service Practices or Businesses to secure the loans (for a lender that typically wants to be over-secured). The problem with early bank financing support, as a part of the SBA rules, was that the lenders required sellers (G1s) to sell all of their equity or assets and to effectively leave the business in order for the buyer to qualify for the loan. Even the presence of a G1's ongoing, post-sale employment agreement was carefully scrutinized by the banks' underwriters and credit analysts. As a result, Seller Financing saved the day ten to fifteen years ago in the first Tranche or two and, on occasion, it still does.

Sellers, or G1s, sometimes still offer to carry the paper on a G2 loan(s) to earn the interest and to offer friendly terms to a G2 or G3 that might need some help financially. Sellers can also offer a variety of unique payment plans, such as interest-only payments for the first year or two, an actual Profit-Based Note as described earlier in this Chapter, a gradually stepped or increasing payment plan, and more. Almost everything can be made to work when the seller is willing to act as the banker.

Fast forward to the present day and many banks now are willing to offer conventional bank financing for five to ten-year terms at competitive rates, and for partial purchases of Equity (think 5%, 10%, 20%, etc.) as is common in the Tranche-by-Tranche Succession Planning process. With the evolution and improvement of banks' handling of

Succession Plan and Exit Plan transactions, Seller Financing is less common today. Seller Financing scenarios tend to be limited to situations where the amount borrowed is less than $100,000, when young, first-time buyers/borrowers are not able to meet a bank's minimum financial requirements or have some large student loans weighing them down, and for significant loans ($750,000+) in an early Tranche. One of the common and important elements of all these Seller Financed loans is that G1 continues to come in to the office most days and is still an active participant in the Business after G2/G3 has bought in.

On occasion, we've seen G1s offer a no down payment, no interest, deferred payment loan to help a younger G2 or G3 complete a first time buy in. Be aware that in such instances the IRS will impute interest on the transaction and can treat the imputed interest as income to the seller even if they haven't actually received any payments. This complicates the tax accounting and turns money that should be taxed as a capital gain into money taxed as ordinary income. G2/G3, you should consult your local tax advisor about these questions before finalizing the financing. The Applicable Federal Rate (AFR), published monthly by the IRS, is the minimum interest rate that the IRS permits for private loans.

G1's motives in providing Seller Financing may not be completely altruistic as the math on this can be compelling. Over a period of up to ten years, during T1, the combination of principal and interest payments, plus G1's wages, and profits, and benefits, and stock appreciation (with G1 continuing to hold a significant Equity Interest as this part of the Plan unfolds) presents a lucrative package. Rather than a lump sum, the Equity Income and interest is spread out much more evenly. G2 and G3, my advice to you is don't be afraid to ask G1 for some help in Tranche One. With that, let's reconsider the concept of Shareholder Value from G1's perspective, adding in the Seller Financing component (emphasis added):

WAGES + PROFIT DISTRIBUTIONS + EQUITY INCOME + <u>INTEREST INCOME</u> + STOCK APPRECIATION

To close this Section out, our standard advice is that Seller Financing makes sense when G1 is in the office, effectively in control, and is in a position to watch over their collateral. The latter Tranches of a Succession Plan should always be bank financed if possible and practical. At some point, you need to let a bank do what a bank does best.

SECTION 5: THE ISSUE OF BASIS

Basis is generally the amount of your capital investment in property for tax purposes. In most situations, the Basis of an asset is equal to what you paid for it, whether with cash, debt obligations, or other property. The issue of **Basis** (also called **Cost Basis**) separately affects G1 owners and G2/G3 owners, with our focus in this Section being on next gen buyers/investors.

Here is why it matters to a G2 or G3 buyer/investor. If you buy an Equity Interest, your Basis is equal to the purchase price. G2, if you purchase 100,000 shares of stock in Newco, LLC for $1.50/share, then your Basis is $150,000. If you then sell those shares for $5.00/share 20 years later, your gain is calculated based on the difference between the sale price and the Basis: $500,000 - $150,000 = $350,000. Absent other factors, the $350,000 is taxed at **Long-Term Capital Gains (LTCG)** rates under the then current **Internal Revenue Code (IRC)**.

In a Succession Plan, Cost Basis matters because it is the starting point for calculating gain or loss on the purchase or sale of stock or Equity. If you sell an Equity Interest in a Professional Services Business for more than its Cost Basis, you will realize a capital gain; if you sell Equity for less than its Cost Basis, you will realize a loss. In certain situations where the Cost Basis can and has been depreciated, the amount between the original Basis and the depreciated Basis is taxed as ordinary income.

Depending on your role, buyer vs. seller, in a Succession Plan, you will experience different impacts. At the G1 ownership level, founders normally have little Basis. This means that as G1 sells their stock, Tranche-by-Tranche, the amount of the proceeds to the seller that exceeds the seller's Basis is fully taxable, commonly at LTCG tax rates. The act of a G1 owner contributing all their rights, title and interest in their Capital Assets into Newco upon set up of the entity does not increase or decrease the amount of Basis that G1, or any other owner for that matter, may have had prior to the contribution. Whatever Basis a person has prior to their contribution is carryover Basis.

The issue of Basis, as it impacts the Successor Team members, is a totally different experience. Focusing on just the next generation of ownership, G2/G3, let's begin with your buying Equity from G1 and financing it with a conventional bank loan amortized over ten years. The principal you have paid creates Basis—so while G1 owners typically have only nominal Basis, G2s and G3s, you may end up with hundreds of thousands of dollars, even millions of dollars of Basis over the full course of the Plan. In the near term, the after-tax cost of the stock when you buy Equity from G1(s) is expensive, but the benefit is that when you and the rest of the Successor Team grow older, perhaps in an era of substantially higher tax rates, you will begin to sell your stock and be able to offset the proceeds against your Cost Basis.

Every shareholder of a Business engaged in a Succession Plan should put their Stock Purchase Agreements, Promissory Notes and related transaction documents, as well as copies of all business valuations or appraisals for each Tranche or purchase in a safe place and hold on to the documents for the rest of their lives. The IRS expects taxpayers to keep the original documentation for Capital Assets and investments; it uses these documents, along with third-party records, bank statements and any published market data, to verify Cost Basis during an audit. Similarly, specific records should be kept of Newco's assets at each buy in or buy out. If those assets have been depreciated, Basis may need to be recaptured at ordinary income rates.

Calculating your Cost Basis is generally pretty straightforward, but something to always be discussed with your local tax advisor. In the course of a Succession Plan where growth fuels the buy-in process, the Plan and the hope is that the stock bought in each Tranche will double in value one or more times during your career, G2/G3, with your help and your thinking. The offsetting Basis will be crucial when you, as a G2 owner, start selling your Equity to the G3 group of owners/investors. Basis is an important part of doing the math when building a sustainable, multi-owner/multi-generational Business, even if its benefits are deferred for a decade or more.

SECTION 6: IT'S A BUY-IN, NOT A BUY-OUT

A Succession Plan tends to unfold incrementally over time in a series of steps, or Tranches as you've learned. Most Succession Plans have two to three Tranches. Some Plans that start earlier (i.e., 20 to 25 years before G1 is ready to retire, for example), or have a lot of next generation ownership talent, might have four or five tranches that move smaller amounts of Equity with greater frequency, but almost always in increments of 5% or more. The only rule is to work within your specific fact pattern to create a Plan that works for all involved. G2/G3, you don't necessarily have to buy Equity in every Tranche. Because of the costs associated with documenting each Tranche and appraising the Business for each Equity purchase/sale, more than five Tranches is rare.

The point is that G2 and any other members of the Successor Team do not buy the entire Practice or Business all at once, nor does a next gen buyer acquire, in most cases, even a controlling interest. The idea is that G2(A) might end up becoming a 40% owner over three Tranches, while G2(B) and G2(C) each become 30% owners over multiple Tranches as well (see *Figure 10*). This slow, steady buy-in/buy-out process is what makes a Succession Plan unique, and appealing to many founding owners. All the owners need to work together over a decade or more and help each other which, in turn, should make the Business much stronger and more valuable than a one-owner Practice model.

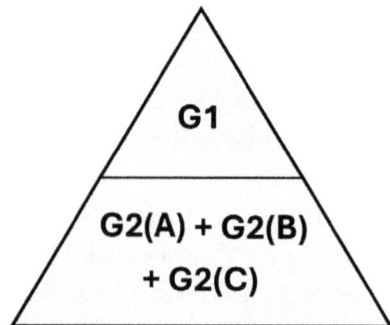

Figure 10

A good Plan design takes into account the current value of the Business, G1's estimated time to full retirement, the Business's anticipated, sustainable growth rate, profitability, and, of course, the talent level, ages, and length of service (LOS) of the G2/G3 level prospective owners. From these basic facts, among others, the overall estimated length of the Plan is then divided into a series of Tranches. Let's assume that G1 is 50 years of age and wants to work another twenty years, slowly reducing work hours over the last half of the Plan. This fact pattern should easily accommodate a three Tranche Plan. If there is more than enough time, as in this example, each Tranche can be completely paid off before the next one starts; if the Plan needs to be condensed to fit a shorter timetable, each Tranche can overlap the previous Tranche as needed.

The first Tranche (T1) is commonly used to initiate, even validate the process and involves the first member(s) of the Successor Team individually acquiring a minority interest in the Business from G1. G1, once convinced that the Plan will work based on actual performance in T1 by the G2/G3 owner(s), may choose to accelerate the Plan prior to completion of T1 and start T2 four or five years into T1, for example, even though the next gen owners may each have a ten-year amortization schedule for T1 via a conventional bank loan (or seller financing). With sufficient growth and profitability, each Tranche ideally should require about 7 to 8 years to pay off using only G2's/G3's pro rata share of profit distributions. A ten-year amortization schedule is designed to provide some cushion to the Equity buyer(s), just in case.

As the Plan is adjusted over time, adapting to actual growth and profitability levels, T3 might overlap T2's amortization schedule, or not. The point is that this approach allows each group of owners to adjust the speed of the Plan collectively based on their needs and abilities, and the Business's growth and success.

Conventional bank financing, if and when available to your specific Professional Services model, will often extend payment terms anywhere from five years at the low end, up to ten years at the high end.

A 120-month amortization schedule, however, illustrates a key point in the succession planning process. Purchasing stock, or Equity, in a growing business on an after-tax basis requires time. It is a slow, methodical process. This extended buy in approach necessitates that G1 begin the overall Succession Plan earlier than most founding owners expect. G2/G3, this is a good conversation starter with a G1 who hasn't started thinking about this concept.

The most common age for G1 to start a formal Succession Plan is around age sixty. The *best age* for G1 to start their Plan is closer to age fifty. More time supports a better, more manageable and gradual Plan. G1 will benefit from the extra time to put together a great Successor Team, which often results in less need to accelerate the Tranches and allows for the occasional misstep along the way (such as a G2 quitting, or underperforming).

Understand that T2 and T3 are not the result of formal contracts, or obligations, on G1 or the G2/G3 owners ahead of time. In other words, G2/G3 owners, you are not obligated to buy a certain amount of stock at some designated point in the future at an unknown price in an unknown economy. The spreadsheet work lays out the architecture for all the Tranches and then serves as a guide to the buyers and sellers, or G1s and G2s/G3s, over the coming years. The spreadsheet model of the Plan is then updated annually and adapted to the realities of the Business. Later in this book, we'll add in the concept of what it means to be good stewards of ownership. Stewardship rules, if and when implemented, can create an impetus for G1 to sell or at least make their Equity available for purchase at certain set times in the future. Absent this approach, after T1, the only legal obligations to buy or sell Equity occur upon a triggering event under the Business's Continuity Plan (i.e., the Buy-Sell Agreement).

SECTION 7: TAX EFFICIENCIES IN A SUCCESSION PLAN

A Succession Plan, and its underlying entity structure specifically, permits owners to build wealth and take money home at a variety of lower tax rates as compared to ordinary income rates under the current IRC. This makes long-term planning and Business building part of the value monetization process. From a G2/G3's perspective, some of your benefits will not be received until after your buy-in is complete and your Equity Interest, starting at around age 50 or so, begins to be gradually monetized in the next edition of the Business's Succession Plan. For now, let's illustrate the benefits of a Succession Plan's tax efficiencies from G1's perspective.

The Shareholder Value concept directly applies to this discussion, with G2 looking ahead to these same benefits in a Business that will hopefully have grown significantly:

WAGES + PROFIT DISTRIBUTIONS + EQUITY INCOME + STOCK APPRECIATION

Let's start this discussion with some important basics. As a sole proprietor or a single owner LLC taxed as a Disregarded Entity (filing one or more Schedule C's attached to your form 1040 in most cases), all the money that flows home from your Book or Practice, after expenses are deducted, is taxed as ordinary income. Effectively, we refer to this as a *two-basket cash flow model* with Basket No. 1 used for general overhead expenses and Basket No. 2 used for wages *and* profits which, in a sole proprietorship, are taxed at the same ordinary income rate.

When setting up a Business to support a Succession Plan, we shift to a Three-Basket Cash Flow model covered earlier in this Chapter, which becomes more impactful as the Business starts to make money from the efforts of others as well (see *Figure 11*).

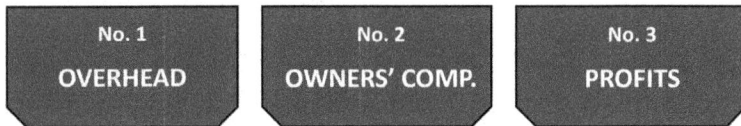

No. 1 OVERHEAD	No. 2 OWNERS' COMP.	No. 3 PROFITS

Figure 11

With the table now set, let's talk about the tax efficiencies assuming that your entity structure includes an S-Corporation (this could be a basic S-Corporation, an LLC electing to be taxed as an S-Corporation, or a Hybrid Entity Structure which utilizes an S-Corporation as a satellite Member of an LLC taxed as a Partnership)—all covered in detail in Chapter Four.

In Tranche One, or T1, the founding owner(s) will receive wages for the work they do (at ordinary income rates), plus profits for the ownership they hold (at slightly less than ordinary income rates) after the first sale in T1, plus sale proceeds at LTCG tax rates less any Basis (i.e., Equity Income) even as the Business continues to grow with the help of the new, next generation owner(s) (stock appreciation). Stock appreciates tax free until one day it is sold and the value is realized. Those are four different tax rates, three at less than ordinary income rates, as money and wealth are created and realized. Of course, the ability to write off business expenses, perhaps both in the primary business office and your home office, adds yet another beneficial layer. And there's more…

Over time, as the Succession Plan moves into T2 and T3, the assumption is that as G1 gets older, they will gradually work fewer hours in the Business. This assumption is based not only on observation and common sense but also on the need to forge a strong Successor Team. In a Succession Plan, the clientele of the Business, as well as the staff members, need to see the G2s and G3s gradually assuming more of the responsibilities. Having G1 spend a little more time out of the office and trusting and training the next generation owners to supervise the operations in G1s absence is a necessary part of the process. It is also an important benefit to G1 that doesn't show up on any spreadsheet—remind them if they forget!

As G1 slowly reduces hours worked, there is a strong tendency for G1's wages (Basket No. 2 in a Three-Basket Cash Flow model) to plateau indefinitely and even, over time, to decline, sometimes offset by a stipend for their role on the Board of Directors (covered in Chapter Six). This is why laying out the details of the Succession Plan cash flow over ten years minimum is so important. In a growing Business, even as G1's wages plateau or decline in the latter Tranches, G1's profit distributions should continue to climb (in actual dollars rather than as a percentage of Equity owned), as well as their stock price since the G2s are using smart, efficient growth to fuel their debt service and investment in the Business. Note that the income stream at the highest tax rate to G1 is the first to be eroded; that's not a coincidence. G1 has other ways, and better ways, to get the money home! G2s and G3s, remember, this is how your own Succession Plan will function one day.

SECTION 8: USING RESIDUAL EQUITY TO YOUR ADVANTAGE

In most Plans, G1 gradually sells their Equity, Tranche-by-Tranche, down to 0.00% ownership at some point. The Successor Team of G2s and G3s are tasked with gradually buying all of G1's Equity even as, especially as, the value and price of the Equity grows. The Equity acquisitions are after-tax and, using a conventional bank loan, with interest. Collectively, this is a very heavy lift, G2/G3, as you've figured out by now. And with fewer members on the Successor Team in some instances, the buy-in process can indeed seem challenging, even overwhelming.

A **Residual Equity** strategy offers a solution, and it provides benefits to all generations of ownership. The strategy lies in G1(s) holding on to some of their Equity into perpetuity, or for the remainder of their natural lives in most cases (possibly tied to a term life insurance policy on their life), at which point the Business redeems G1's remaining interest and cashes out their estate at FMV at that moment in time. In sum, G1 doesn't sell all of their Equity in the course of their working career and prior to their full retirement. As a G2/G3 owner, you don't have to buy out all the founder's Equity, at least not within the typical retirement time horizon. Residual Equity can change the timing rules in a meaningful way.

A typical Residual Equity strategy might allow G1 to continue to own up to 10% to 20% of the issued and outstanding shares of the Business, and to continue to benefit from any associated profit distributions and stock appreciation rights. Conversely, G2/G3 does not have to worry about buying and financing all of G1's stock, especially if they're still paying off a loan on the previous Tranche(s). And as the Business's entire client base tacitly observes the Business Succession Plan unfolding and witnesses G1's gradual on-the-job retirement in favor of a younger Successor Team, it can be beneficial to tell the existing clients, and even prospective clients, that the founder is still an owner of the Business.

More likely than not, G1, once in the Residual Equity phase of the Succession Plan, will either drop off the payroll completely or take a reduced wage as part of their buy out, and may give up the proverbial corner office, or not. Some businesses find real value in providing an office to a senior member who is no longer an active producer or service provider. The value lies in having these senior owners and team members spend unpaid time in the office providing guidance and wisdom to the next generations of PSP's and owners. Residual Equity often helps G1 stay just enough involved to make retirement less of a sudden stop and to provide some long-term growth benefits and upside. This strategy can also be used to find the additional time that might be needed to onboard another member to the Successor Team to help buy out this last block of Equity.

Some Professional Service Business models, if regulated and needing licensure to deliver services, may not be allowed to have a residual owner unless that person retains licensure in all states where the Business has clients and, in many cases, E&O (Errors & Omissions insurance) or malpractice insurance coverage. Sometimes these costs are material and sometimes not. The financial services world where I come from, for instance, has regulatory provisions for certain licensees that would not allow a non-licensed individual to share in a Business's profit distribution dollars once they relinquish licensure. This is something to verify given your Professional Services venue.

Finally, many of the clients I have consulted with to design and implement a Succession Plan start too late, or a little later than optimum. In fact, starting late is more the norm than not! I'm not piling on here. The point is that a shortened timetable can be rectified by using a Residual Equity strategy. Suddenly, the Business and the next generation owners have an extra five to ten years, perhaps, to work with and G1 has some additional upside and a way to stay involved even if limited to cheering on the team from the near sidelines.

Lessons To Be Learned

- T1 is the hardest part of a Succession Plan—worst case, Seller Financing can make the math work out.

- Profitability and growth directly impact the value of a Business, as well as how investable it is.

- The term "profit distributions" is appropriate for S-Corporations and flow-through LLC entity structures; the term "dividend" is associated with a C-Corporation and reflects the unique tax and cash flow aspects of that specific entity.

- Cash flow should be compartmentalized into three groups (overhead, owners' compensation, and profits) and tracked on an annual basis to determine performance, enhance value, and to support G2/G3's equity purchases and financing.

- Seller financing and conventional bank financing are both used to support next generation investment into a Business. Seller financing is the most flexible approach and is used primarily in the first Tranche.

- The concept of "Shareholder Value" [wages + profits + equity income + stock appreciation] demonstrates the broad package of ownership benefits to PSPs willing to bear the risk of ownership.

- Residual Equity strategies can reshape the timeframe for a Succession Plan and provide substantial benefits to all owners.

Defined Terms in the Order Presented in this Chapter

- Return on Investment (ROI)
- Three-Basket Cash Flow System
- Equity Blueprint
- Tranche One (T1)
- Fair Market Value (FMV)
- Tranche Two (T2)
- Equity Income
- Seller Financing
- Profit-Based Note
- Performance Ratios
- Plateau Level Compensation Strategy
- Cost of Living Adjustment (COLA)
- Basis (or Cost Basis)
- Long Term Capital Gains (LTCG)
- Internal Revenue Code (IRC)
- Residual Equity

CHAPTER THREE:
A TEAM BUILT FOR THE AGES

The most basic Succession Plan begins with two generations of owners, a G1 and a G2. Sometimes this is a parent and a son or a daughter, and sometimes this is a group of three founders who empower a next generation team of three new and younger ownership prospects. Regardless, as a Business grows, the ranks of owners and support personnel should grow as well, in every sense of that word. The process should be gradual, purposeful, and powerful—a team built for the ages.

SECTION 1: WHAT DOES IT MEAN TO BUILD A LEGACY?

In the decades I've been doing this, I often ask the founders to answer one question right up front: "How does your story end?" G2/G3, one day, that same question will be asked of you. I hear lots of different answers but one of my favorite is "I want to build a legacy," except that when I ask what that means to them, specifically, I learn that it means something slightly different to almost every owner and entrepreneur.

Some G1s want to build a business that will outlive them. Some feel a commitment to ensure their work and their advice continues on and is delivered by a trained team who can carry on a certain culture. To others, I hear about an implied promise to always be there and to get the job done on the clients' timeline, not within the PSPs career boundaries.

I think that a **Business Legacy Model** entails something more than just a business that carries on through succeeding generations of ownership, though that is a part of the answer. It is more than a Succession Plan to a founder. I think that it includes not only a transfer of ownership but also a transfer of knowledge, experience, and a culture—the special way that the founding generation got the work done and delivered great services. I used to think that family businesses had a clear edge on Legacy building but through experience and observation, I now think that family-like businesses hold the edge. Regardless, here is a working list of what constitutes a Business Legacy Model from my perspective:

(a) A Professional Services Business should prioritize delivering ongoing services with consistent core values to the next generation, beginning with the clients;

(b) The services need to be delivered under a continuous or similar business name and in, or from, the same general geographical area;

(c) The services need to gradually and continually improve while safeguarding the Business's reputation in the community;

(d) The business needs to be adaptable and resilient, changing with the times, the economy, the rules and regulations, and client demands;

(e) The business and its ownership team needs to give back to the community that it serves;

(f) A client cannot purchase the same services from someone else around the corner from a Legacy business—therefore, a Legacy business needs to deliver something more, something different, often cited as a continuation of a certain culture, but also with a built-in culture of continuation.

These are thoughts, not rules. Of course there are exceptions. But when you next talk to G1, your boss(s), about what they want to do with the Business at the end of their career, listen carefully to their thoughts and any inference that they'd like to create a Legacy because it means something more than just passing the Business on to new owners or key employees and getting bought out. It might mean something special and distinct to them and you need to understand what that is, and what your role in that process might be. It almost certainly means something more than building a profitable, valuable, investable and sustainable Business.

G1 starts it all, but there is no Legacy without long-tenured, key employees and next gen owners who are trained in the processes of service delivery and can pass along that training, with improvements, to future employees and owners. Leadership from one generation to the next must carry the burden of respecting and remembering the past while adapting to the present and making sure the clients never forget what makes a Legacy business different and special. It isn't easy. It takes a special team of people all working together. Legacy or not, that is what this Chapter is all about.

SECTION 2: DEVELOPING A SUCCESSOR TEAM

A Succession Plan involves multiple owners and multiple generations of ownership who work together to build a valuable, growing, and sustainable Business. The basic formula to support this process is: G1 + G2 + G3, or more precisely, G1 + G2(x2) + G3(x3) (see *Figure 12*). Each generation of ownership tends to require a gradually broader base of ownership to support the buy-in costs of the more senior generation of owners in a growing business.

As you now know, G2 and G3, it is not necessary to have a full generation between each level of ownership such as with a parent and a son or daughter. It is, however, important to understand that the math of a Succession Plan requires, or at least benefits from, a separation of about 12 to 15 years from the selling owner(s) to the next level of ownership. The issue is that a

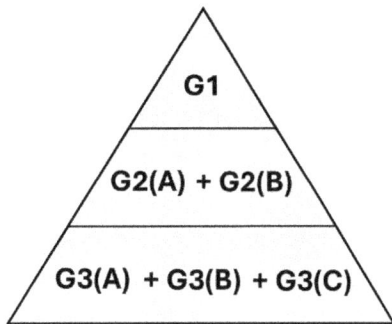

Figure 12

G2 close in age to a G1 approaching retirement likely will not have sufficient time to fulfill a multi-Tranche plan and may not be willing to incur long-term debt to fund G1's sale of Equity.

If the Succession Plan starts when G1 is 53 years of age, the basic math (including amortization schedules to support the after-tax Equity buy in process) suggests that two prospective next generation owners should ideally be in their mid to late 30s to provide the best results. If G2(A) is 34 and G2(B) is 38, the G2s average age of 36 is used for planning and modeling purposes. This is about a 17 year average age difference compared to G1, in this simple example. Of course, there are other factors that come into play, so the math for each generational level of the Plan depends on your specific situation. Succession Plans are custom designed and built to address each Business's specific fact pattern and goals.

The exact number of G2 owners and G3 owners depends on the goals, timeframe, profitability level, growth rates and the value of the Business—and of course the pool of available next gen talent. The **Successor Team** is commonly composed of two or more younger owners who collectively (but not always equally) purchase ownership from the G1 level. In most cases, the process starts with a single key employee whose length of service (LOS) with the subject Business is at least three to four years (the issue of Tenure is covered in the following Section). It may be several years later that G1, while working with an existing G2, adds a second member to the Successor Team, and so on.

A good general guideline is two G2s for every owner in the G1 position, a pattern loosely repeated for the G3s who will be tasked with being the Successor Team for the broader base of G2 owners. That said, two or three G2s can typically buy out two G1s in most cases. Avoid having just one G2, or one person, on your Successor Team whose task is to buy out one G1; it can work, but there is no room for error and the debt load, even when spread out over time, on one individual buyer can be overwhelming and may result in a price paid that is lower, perhaps much lower, than Fair Market Value (FMV).

To further the case for multiple next gen PSPs, let's revisit the Continuity Plan process and provide more context. Businesses use a Buy-Sell Agreement to address sudden changes in the ownership team (death, disability, termination of employment status, loss of licensure, etc.). Consider the possibility that, if four or five years into Tranche One (T1) of the Succession Plan, after the Business has grown significantly, G1 has to buy out their only G2 because that G2 owner has a serious health issue or accident, or just doesn't want to pursue an Equity path any longer. This Succession Plan has just shifted into reverse. G1 is now buying Equity instead of selling it. The better approach is that each G2 owner needs to participate in a Continuity Plan that relies on other G2 owners. Beyond age 50, or so, it makes no sense for G1 (or any of the senior owners), to be acquiring Equity from the younger owners, or any owner for that matter, if Succession Planning is the goal.

A new Human Resources or HR Team also tends to emerge from this process. As the Succession Plan gradually unfolds, and certainly by the time G2(s) acquire more Equity in T2 (Tranche Two), the responsibility for hiring, training and promoting next generation talent should begin to shift to the senior Successor Team members, with guidance from G1(s) of course. The G3 level of ownership will be the future Business and continuity partners for G2, so it is important to let the G2 owners make some of these decisions, right or wrong; it's part of being an owner.

To this end, founding owners often struggle to find enough qualified, next generation talent to support their Plan. The concern is often expressed as "How do I find people who will work as hard and care as much about my Business as I do?" which, in fairness, is a good question that must be asked and answered. In a growing and evolving Business, however, the idea is that a team of next generation owners, each doing what they do best, can cumulatively succeed and supplant the entrepreneurial model where the founder does all or most of the important work whether they are really good at it or not. G1 is replaced by the cumulative talents and efforts of the Successor Team with G1 moving from entrepreneur, to CEO, to Chairperson of the

Board, to mentor, retiring when they and the Business and client base are ready. Over the decades, I've often been pleasantly surprised, and occasionally shocked, at the level of success and ingenuity these Successor Teams can generate.

Finally, let's address ownership prospects who are non-revenue producers and non-service providers. G2 owners, eventually the senior members of the Successor Team, are almost always revenue producers because revenue growth is largely where the money comes from to fuel the debt service on the Equity purchases. Non-revenue producers who play a key role in the Business such as a Chief Compliance Officer or a Chief Marketing Officer, for example, can certainly be owners as well but tend to be smaller owners (think 3% to 5% of the total ownership picture) and often opt instead for a Synthetic Equity solution (Phantom Stock, Stock Appreciation Rights, a Profits Interest, etc., covered in Chapter Nine) that provides a wealth building opportunity with no debt service obligation.

But don't assume anything. If you have a loyal, hardworking key employee who really makes a difference and is in it for the long term, it just might make sense to have a conversation and talk about the opportunity and see what they think.

SECTION 3: THE ISSUE OF TENURE

The issue of tenure stems from a common question, and concern, expressed by founding owners of their key employees, sons and daughters—"How long should my G2s and G3s have to work for me before they're ready for ownership?" For the most part, this is a **Length of Service (LOS)** issue, even though tenure can and should consider other aspects of an employee's long-term relationship with a particular business or employer. To this end, the concern expressed by G1 is commonly "How soon is too soon?," only to be followed years later by "Oh, I guess I waited too long." In fairness, these questions are reserved for the best of the next generation PSPs.

When working through this issue with the G1 level of ownership, I rephrase the question for them as this: "So how do you get a 30-something-year-old (plus or minus ten years), minority owner of an intangible, Professional Services Business to make the first of a series of career-length investments? And then to do it again, and maybe again?!" The fact is that not all thirty-something year old G2s or G3s will stick with it. Some won't even start. Ownership, along with the opportunities and obligations that come with it, is not for everyone. In fairness, we're talking about the single, longest commitment a young, first time owner will make, next to their marriage. Even a thirty-year home mortgage allows for a complete change of residence, or two, or three, along the way. The answer to G1's question is not numerical; it depends on the circumstances and the person (G2/G3).

G2/G3, you need a certain amount of time to get ready and to make this commitment and while the amount of time varies by individual and by the opportunity, I think there is a minimum threshold to consider.

Starting with the end in mind, let's work back to explain how to best address the tenure or LOS issue. Perhaps ten to twenty years after a Succession Plan begins, the next generation owners may well have an ownership structure, after G1 retires, of 40%/30%/30%, for example. This structure supports three next gen owners, all with minority ownership positions, all with seats on the Board of Directors (covered in Chapter Six). From this ownership structure, the process of continuity planning and implementing a third generation of successors becomes much more manageable than buying out a 100%, dominant G1 owner, for example. The journey from the first generation to the second generation is the most challenging because, in any given Business, it has never been done. The journey from the second generation to the third, and even a fourth generation theoretically, has a blueprint to follow, and a culture of continuation to guide it.

Also consider that the 40% owner in our example will probably acquire their total Equity Interest over two or three Tranches. This reduces the total investment per Tranche and gives each member of the Successor Team the opportunity to reassess the opportunity at hand, along with their spouse or significant other. Is there a good reason to buy more Equity? Does the ROI justify the rising Equity price (the answer to which, at some point, becomes G2's responsibility)? Looking to the future, is the growth and profitability of the Business sufficient, and sustainable, to support the investment? Should the Business at issue be sold off to an even larger Business? These are questions to be weighed by increasingly experienced next generation investors as the Succession Plan progresses. They're the right questions to be asking.

The Successor Team isn't obligated to acquire more Equity if they don't think it is wise or it is too risky. This isn't one, single, large investment—it is a series of smaller ones with the time to carefully consider each step. But multiple Tranches, if that is how it works out, take time. In turn, it takes a strong, well-run Business over many years for the Successor Team members to make it through this gauntlet. Along the way, a G2's Equity Interest very quickly becomes the single, largest, most valuable asset they own, and it is an asset that they are helping to grow—G2s begin to have some real control over their own future and wealth.

So here is a more direct answer to the question, "How long should you, as a G2 or G3 prospect, have to work for or in a Business before you're ready for ownership?" Many Professional Service Businesses lean toward the six to nine-year or seven to ten-year levels of continuous service and employment at a given Business, borrowing a concept from the legal and tax professions I think. That works for many Professional Service Businesses, but a better approach in my experience is to establish a Length of Service framework (not a set of rules) centered on the answers to these questions:

- What is G1's overall timeframe and specific plan?
- When is each G2/G3 prospect ready to make a career length commitment and sign up for a ten-year amortized, personal loan for this opportunity?
- How hard would it be to replace a key employee/G2/G3

prospect if they left for a better opportunity or another ownership opportunity with a lower LOS requirement?

Current and prospective owners should prioritize specific goals and circumstances over traditional rules.

A preceding LOS for a G2 or a G3 prospective owner of three to five years is on the faster side, with four to six years probably being closer to the right answer for most Professional Service owners. As a young lawyer, I remember being told that the unofficial *LOS rules* where I interned were seven to nine years, and if I didn't hear anything by end-of-year nine, don't bother asking! Rules are rules. Frankly, that was too long for me so I left and *hung out my own shingle*, and I had a lot of attorney colleagues who did the same or found other employment.

G2 and G3, if you're talented enough, smart enough, and motivated enough to take on the risk of being an owner, break the rules! Start the conversation. After reading this book, you may well know more about the process than the founding owners, or your boss. Change has to begin with someone.

SECTION 4: FAMILY MEMBERS ON THE PAYROLL

In my consulting work with a new Succession Planning client, a question that must always be asked, with one question leading to another, is this: "Are there any family members currently on the payroll?" And, if so, "Do those family members actually work in the business on a full time or a part time basis?" And, if so, "Do they receive a compensation package equivalent to a non-family member?" And then it's time to just listen.

The answers don't matter much in a one-owner Practice, but it does start to matter a lot when new owners/investors think about buying-in and they look over the Profit & Loss Statement. The good news is that there is almost always a workable solution for this particular expense item. A lot of Book and Practice owners have a family member on the payroll, and that can bleed over into a Business as well. To be clear, G2/G3 readers, this Section is not about family members becoming owners—that issue is addressed in Chapter Seven. This is more about G1 taking care of their own.

G2/G3, this is written to help you address or work through this issue if it is, or could be a problem. To figure out how to best handle the issue, both financially and emotionally in many cases, let's put our three cash flow baskets back on the table. To refresh your memory, Basket No. 1 is for general overhead, Basket No. 2 is reserved for owners' compensation, and Basket No. 3 is for profits. When a family member of an owner is on the payroll, they usually get paid out of Basket No. 1. From a Business perspective, they are expenses. In an Equity-Centric Business model, however, they should be shifted to Basket No. 2 and tucked underneath their spouse or significant other, the G1 owner(s). In other words, G1's total wages for the work they do *will include* what they want or need to share with their significant other or family member. This works fairly well provided it does not compromise or erode the profitability level of Basket No. 3.

To this end, one of the first tasks a Financial Analyst will attend to when modeling a Succession Plan is to create a base year P&L Statement using the **trailing twelve months** revenue, or a **T-12** P&L. Performance Ratios, used to track the changing levels of the Three-Basket Cash Flow System from year-to-year, are projected based on anticipated expenses, growth and efficiencies from the base year P&L. If the cash flow system starts out at 50%/40%/10%, for example, changes will need to be swift and certain or the G2/G3 investment(s) may not happen. The Performance Ratios may not support an investment opportunity. If, on the other hand, the Performance Ratios reflect a frugal business operation and the base year is around 50%/25%/25% or 50%/20%/30%, all issues are open to consideration and adjustment; these Ratio levels might be very competitive depending on the norms for your Professional Services Venue.

The good and general rule here is that, in a Professional Services Business, people on the payroll need to come in to work or, if one is working from home, put in a full work day. If a founder doesn't like that change as it applies to them, another possible solution might be the Hybrid Entity Structure outlined in Chapter Four, which allows an owner to handle their own personal payroll through their private LLC/S-Corporation satellite Member. The other owners can do the same thing if they like.

Culturally, having spouses (and/or younger children) on the payroll of a small business with multiple owners and generations of ownership is difficult, sometimes *even if* they work in the Business. The clock on their involvement immediately starts to tick upon G2's entrance. It has to. G2/G3, let me say it for you: "G1, don't blame the next generation owners; as smart investors, they have to learn to pay close attention to the profitability level and, accordingly, seek to eliminate or reduce inefficiencies. That's a good thing." G2/G3 owners who put their houses on the line for this career-length opportunity may go along with the founder's pleasures for a while, but lifestyle Practices don't tend to last or warrant significant investment, or grow into valuable, sustainable Businesses. G2/G3, you need to know this going in and make it a part of your due diligence. Maybe you end up with a handshake agreement that in 24 or 36 months, or at the start of T2, all family members come off the payroll.

In fairness, Businesses are built to take care of their owners and the owners' families in addition to employees and clients. The process simply demands more formality when investors and bankers look over the operations. Accept that this change is a part of the process of building a valuable, profitable, sustainable Business.

SECTION 5: ASSEMBLING A PROFESSIONAL SUPPORT TEAM

G2/G3, assembling a professional support team to partner with is an important part of the solution set in setting up a formal Succession Plan, but it is one that you will mostly inherit at least as to the first group (a, b, and c) listed below.

Most Equity-Centric Businesses that successfully implement a multi-Tranche Succession Plan gross over $1.0 million a year, if not at the start, certainly early in the process. At that point, if not well before, most owners have a professional team around them which includes the following:

(a) Accountant

(b) Bookkeeper

(c) Business Attorney

These same professionals can help a founder transition their Book or Practice into a Business with multiple owners, to later be joined by the additional following professionals in the design and implementation of a Succession Plan:

(d) Consultant/Succession Plan Designer

(e) Financial Analyst

(f) Appraiser

Bank Liaison (or someone who's been with the bank awhile such as a private banker)

G2/G3, you may well choose to find your own banking liaison, analyst and appraiser in support of your buy-in process and to help the process along. Collectively, this "group of seven" is your succession planning **Support Team**. After Tranche One, or T1 is implemented, most of the work by the Consultant and Financial Analyst will be completed, leaving open the need for some fine tuning of your Plan over time as it evolves and you learn—but the support team quickly drops to five key players. Your Support Team might be local, and they might not be. In today's world, it is just as likely that you will work with an experienced Financial Analyst or Appraiser on the other side of the country—it really doesn't matter if they're good at what they do.

G2/G3, your Support Team, whatever their talent and experience level and regardless of where they're located, needs to understand and have experience with more than just a basic Business model. As a Professional Services Provider (PSP), it really helps to have an

Accountant and a business Attorney that serve other clients just like you and in your specific line of work or profession. You don't want your Business to be their largest client (as good as that may sound) or the first and only client in your specific field for your tax and legal counsel to practice on—and the only way you'll know is to ask. Of course, early on, these are G1's questions and determinations to make. These professionals each tend to support all owners in the Plan and their invoices are generally paid by the Business.

Just about every Succession Plan I've worked on that has turned out well has involved a Financial Analyst. You just can't fake the math, and you cannot document the Plan without having a complete, detailed and forward looking spreadsheet of the Plan. This is not a requiem for determining who is most important on your Support Team; it is more about the order of things to come, and tax planning and legal documentation follow the detailed analytics.

Let's talk more about the Financial Analyst as a member of your Support Team. This is generally not a CPA function or skill set, and certainly not that of an Attorney. Sometimes, G2/G3, this task falls to you if you have the skills, time and interest—by the time you get to the fifth or sixth draft, you'll likely have it figured out! The Financial Analyst team member is tasked with modeling on a pro forma basis your specific variables using current and anticipated cash flow models, year-by-year, and Tranche-by-Tranche, accounting for all the owners or possible owner/investors along with debt service and tax impact, using projected but conservative growth rates, salaries (i.e., Basket No. 2), profitability levels, and more.

Appraisers ultimately help you determine business value and produce an appraisal report specific to the purpose at hand; it is the Analyst who will help you determine the actual sales price of the Equity Interest—perhaps the appraised value, perhaps not. This pro forma spreadsheet process, managed well, becomes *the Plan*, and it serves as a guide for all the owners and prospects and is readily adjusted as circumstances warrant over time. As a result, the spreadsheet can also function as an informal Term Sheet or Letter of Intent. Once the spreadsheet is designed and laid out for T1, one or more Successor Team members tend to take over and adjust it for the realities of the Business over time.

Once the pro forma modeling is finished, the next most important person on the team is your local CPA or tax advisor. The Financial Analyst and/or Consultant will need to go review the Plan with your local tax counsel so that city/county/state/federal taxes are taken into consideration for the Business and for all the individual owners. At this point, everything from the entity structure to the compensation plan is considered in a cash flow and tax context. After the Accountant signs off, a business Attorney (often with an M&A background) takes over and will work with a bank loan officer to coordinate and complete all the documentation for the Plan.

Careful attention needs to be paid to the legal process and an Attorney's job to zealously advocate for their specific client. The point is, G2/G3, there is often just one attorney to draft the documents and they are paid by the Business , with checks signed by G1 level owners. That doesn't mean the process can't be fair and impartial, but you need to be aware of the possibilities. The problem is that if all the owners *arm up* with their own, separate legal counsel to battle to the finish, it can be hard to come back to the office and work as collegial business partners later on. Perhaps you hire your own attorney to review documents and counsel only you, privately. Listen to the legal counsel selected by G1 and on behalf of the business and make your own decision.

SECTION 6: NO BOOK BUILDERS ALLOWED

A team built for the ages all work together on the same business, from one generation to the next, helping each other grow and improve what they have collectively invested in. Book builders work for themselves.

Building separate Books can undermine the entire Business building process. These individuals own their Books and any value associated with it. Accordingly, there is no singular, business value for a *group* of Book builders. As a Practice grows into a Business, individual, internal

Book building must end. Book building operations, unfortunately, are not always easy to see.

Before proceeding further, I realize that there are many different Professional Service venues, or occupations, and this may not be a universal problem. If this isn't an issue for you, and you're sure, please proceed to the next Chapter. If there is even a chance that some of the PSPs in the Practice or Business you're thinking of buying into might be thinking that they own the clients they serve or, perhaps, G2/G3, you have a Book of your own, please read on.

Here are the important basics to understand about this issue. Accounting, law, independent financial services, and insurance-based Practices, just to name a few of the Professional Services, are typically operated under a single trade name or DBA. From a leased office space that presents a single identity or trade name to the public, a Practice is often supported by one or more individuals within each office location who are building their own Books. The Book builders, who own their own clients and cash flow, often share office space, a receptionist, a phone and computer system with the Practice owner; they may even share revenue, but they do not share clients other than some joint case work.

Many Professional Service Practices tend to utilize or support this common, simple starting point for newer, younger associates. Basically, in a Practice model where clients are the medium of value (as opposed to Equity or shares of stock), the goal of an incoming associate or contractor or intern is to "go get more clients" and, of course, generate some revenue. Many Book builders start out by helping older or more established PSPs with their client base. Depending on your Professional Services venue, some next generation professionals don't survive or don't excel at this process, and that's the point. Those who are good at getting a client base established, and good enough at the services they provide, are the "keepers." Practices are the testing grounds for these aspiring Book builders.

But this isn't a cautionary tale. This is all about finding talent where it is and enlisting the Book builders' support in building a Business and being part of the Successor Team—if that is at all possible.

One of the biggest challenges to implementing a Succession Plan is finding the necessary talent to work hard and make the monetary investment. Where do you find those people? You need to look at the other side of this coin. I'd argue that the right people, PSPs with ownership experience, are all around you, at least in the Professional Service venues I'm familiar with. There are typically more Book builders, i.e., sole proprietorships, than Practice and Business owners combined. A twenty or thirty-something year old Book owner, perhaps the G2s/G3s reading this Section, can agree to join an existing Business via a tax-neutral exchange (defined in the next Chapter) and become an equity owner without having to buy Equity initially and take on debt service, if the Business sets up the appropriate entity. In effect, G2/G3, if you have your own Book of clients, you can contribute that to a Business in exchange for Equity, effectively adding value by joining a Business and being part of its Successor Team.

My past advice to today's G1 owners, and current advice to tomorrow's G2/G3 owners, is to cultivate two streams of talent for possible future ownership. One is the tried and tested method of hiring, training and rewarding home grown talent. Put these folks on the payroll and nurture them. Share the culture of ownership and business perpetuation. The other way is to cultivate established Book builders. Most Book owners operate as sole proprietors which means that they operate a two-basket cash flow system (overhead expenses in one basket, and wages/profits combined in the second basket) and they may not intuitively understand the benefits of being an Equity owner. Share the concept of Shareholder Value and how your well-structured Business can help a Book owner build greater wealth over time as a member of the Successor Team.

Lessons To Be Learned

- Strong, valuable, successful Businesses require a Successor Team and a Support Team. G2/G3, you may inherit many of these professionals initially as a new owner in a Practice or a Business.

- The basic formula for the Support Team is: $G1 + G2 + G3$, or more precisely, $G1 + G2(x2) + G3(x3)$. Each generation of ownership tends to utilize a gradually broader base of ownership to support the acquisition costs of buying Equity from the more senior generation of owners.

- In terms of tenure, a preceding Length of Service (LOS) for a G2 or a G3 prospective owner of three to five years is on the faster side, with four to six years probably being closer to the right answer for most Professional Service owners.

- Book building is a natural part of being a Professional Services Provider, or PSP. It can either erode Business value, or add significant value and talent to a Business depending on the circumstances and how it is handled.

- Performance Ratios refer to the process of tracking a Business's general overhead, the total compensation of the ownership team, and the remaining profitability on an annual basis over time. This recommended process derives from the Three-Basket Cash Flow System as a cash management strategy.

Defined Terms in the Order Presented in this Chapter

- Business Legacy Model
- Successor Team
- Length of Service (or LOS)
- Trailing Twelve Months (or T-12)
- Support Team

CHAPTER FOUR: EXAMINING THE ESSENTIAL ENTITY FRAMEWORK

In many cases, as a next gen PSP, you may have little control over the choice of the entity structure you buy into. So why does this matter then to a reader of this book? It is fair to say that many, if not most, G1s did not set up their entity for the purpose of supporting a long-term Succession Plan. This means that as a G2/G3 prospective buyer and investor, you need to have a thorough understanding of how the mechanics of this part of the process work, and how G1's current entity structure might be adapted to make it work better for these purposes. This area is a major part of your due diligence.

SECTION 1: ENTITY STRUCTURING BASICS

I like to start my succession planning workshops out by explaining that an entity structure is akin to the concrete footings put into place when building a new home. It is one of the very first steps in the building process, and arguably the most important. The concrete footings and stem walls, mostly below ground level, provide rigidity and load-bearing strength. Every part of the house is in one way or another attached to or supported by this solid foundation, built to last for generations. Generally, when the home is complete and ready for occupancy by the owners, these concrete support elements are mostly hidden from sight and barely noticed, but there is no house without this critical functional part of the whole. The same is true of the underlying entity structure in support of a Succession Plan.

Remember that a Succession Plan starts with a transfer of Capital Assets and value from individual producers or service providers into the entity. The entity then issues Equity as shares of stock or units in exchange to each contributing owner. The founding owner(s) can then sell a portion of their Equity to next generation owners or prospective investors—that's you, G2/G3. These are the basic workings of a Succession Plan. Stock can be transferred, for value, in increments as small as one share, but more commonly in 5%, 10%, or 20% increments to start a Succession Plan. If 1,000,000 shares of stock are authorized and issued, for example, then we're talking about you buying 50,000 shares to 200,000 shares per Tranche. This is why an entity serves as the foundation for the Plan—it provides for incremental transfer of value in a single business.

Some entities such as C-Corporations and LLC's taxed as Partnerships can issue more than one class of stock, but in almost every case, Professional Service Businesses setting up a Succession Plan only need one class of Equity. A second class may be needed at some point in the future, but often not until business value is at $10.0 million, or more. An entity can generally authorize and issue as many shares of stock as it wishes; we'll provide some specific recommendations and more logic in a later Section of this Chapter. As a general rule, however, start on the high side (100,000 shares minimum or, preferably 1,000,000 shares or more—but not 10, or 100 shares which will need to be adjusted later on). Authorizing a larger number of shares initially provides flexibility for future growth, employee incentives, and potential mergers/tax-neutral exchanges/acquisitions.

The underlying entity needed to support a Succession Plan should be a **Tax-Conduit** or flow-through entity structure in which all profit and loss flows through to the owners, pro rata. In such instances, the entity is not considered to be a tax payer, at least federally. Professional Service Businesses capable of producing an elevated level of profitability and flowing these profits pro rata into the hands of its founder(s) and next generation owners helps to address many of the issues for those who are considering the investment risk of a minority ownership position.

Given the strong recommendation and common practice of using some form of a Tax-Conduit structure, the use of a C-Corporation is not recommended. It is possible, of course, that the founder(s) may currently be operating as a C-Corporation because no one thought to make a Subchapter S election or because a choice was made to accumulate assets within the corporation rather than flowing the profits pro rata to the owners. If this is the case, a C-Corporation can subsequently change and make an S-Corporation election, but to avoid recapture tax there is an exclusion period—something to talk to local tax counsel about in advance of making such a change. Very few Equity-Centric Businesses implementing a Succession Plan are structured as a C-Corporation because it is not tax efficient for the purposes of these strategies.

The use of a Limited Liability Company, or LLC, is an increasingly prevalent choice among Professional Service owners because it is an exceptionally flexible and fluid structure. In effect, an LLC can change its underlying tax election, or status, from that of a sole proprietorship, to a Partnership, to a C-Corporation, to an S-Corporation over time as explained in the next Section. For this reason, if a choice exists as to an entity and you or the founders are not absolutely sure of the best course of action, an LLC is the place to start.

Additional benefits of setting up an appropriate entity include:

- Added formality and predictability as operations shift to a multi-owner, multi-generational business model
- A clear and effective governance structure supported by Officers, Directors, shareholders, and employees
- The ability to "onboard" or merge smaller Book owners into the entity via a Tax-Neutral Exchange process
- Limited liability for the equity owners in certain situations

Corporations and LLCs both offer limited liability benefits. Limited liability is always good for an owner, but it often doesn't work quite the same for a Professional Services owner in a regulated business as it does for the owner of a manufacturing firm, for example. Generally, the owners of a properly structured and maintained entity are not personally liable for business debts or contracts. Professional Service owners may, however, remain liable for their own negligence and for any obligations for which they've signed a personal guarantee. The combination of an entity that offers limited liability plus Errors & Omissions (E&O) insurance provides the best protection.

In terms of supporting a Succession Plan, the best underlying entity structure options for most Professional Service Businesses come down to these choices in most states, with each choice explained in more detail later in this Chapter:

(a) An LLC that elects to be taxed as either a Partnership or as an S-Corporation

(b) A Corporation making an S-Corporation tax election

(c) A hybrid model that utilizes an LLC/Partnership as the main, Equity-Centric Business (into which all revenue is deposited) with a supporting satellite Member S-Corporation or LLC/S-Corporation for each owner

Other choices may include, depending on the state you are located in and the type of Professional Service being offered, a PC (Professional Corporation), a PSC (which refers to either a Personal Service Corporation or a Professional Service Corporation, depending on the venue), or a PLLC (a Professional Limited Liability Company). Most states limit the type of people who may create and own a PC, PSC, or PLLC. Generally, these individuals include accountants, engineers, physicians and other healthcare professionals, lawyers, and veterinarians. A Professional Corporation is governed by state law, and states have restrictions which may require a majority of the ownership to be in the hands of licensees or may prohibit unlicensed owners altogether. In most cases, a PC or PLLC can be used to support a Succession

Plan provided the owners can meet their state's specific rules and their licensing board's regulations.

SECTION 2: THE BENEFITS OF A LIMITED LIABILITY COMPANY

A Limited Liability Company (or LLC) is considered by most attorneys and accountants to be the most flexible and fluid type of entity and this general choice tends to be favored as a result. LLC's can also be a bit complicated, in my experience, having been an owner of one for over 25 years. Here is what to know as a G2/G3 prospective owner as you perform your **Due Diligence** to learn more about exactly what you might be investing in.

An LLC comes to life when *Articles of Organization* are filed with the Secretary of State, most commonly in the state where the Business's primary office is located. From this point on, as long as the annual renewal fee is paid, the state will recognize the Business as an LLC or Limited Liability Company. Once the Articles have been approved, an **Employer Identification Number (EIN)** can be obtained through the IRS's online portal and a bank account can be opened. That's the easy stuff. Once an LLC is filed and these basics have been attended to, the founding owner or owners can then choose, as a group, to have the LLC taxed in one of the following four ways:

1. a DE, or Disregarded Entity (if there is only one owner)
2. a Partnership (if there are two or more owners)
3. a C-Corporation, or
4. an S-Corporation

As a prospective owner, you may well have missed the LLC set up and initial tax election, but maybe not—this is indeed a very flexible structure. This tax election process, along with the ability to subsequently change the election under certain circumstances over the coming years as the Business needs change, is why an LLC is often the preferred choice. With a single filing, your LLC can be whatever the ownership group needs it to be, within the bounds of the law and tax code. As a result, there is almost no good reason not to set up an

LLC as the basic or initial structure. The nomenclature used in this book to refer to an LLC that elects to be taxed as a DE, Partnership, or S-Corporation, is simply **LLC/DE**, **LLC/Partnership**, or **LLC/S-Corporation**, respectively.

The election of tax treatment is made solely with the IRS, and then each state in which the Business operates will recognize the entity as such. If there is one owner of an LLC, it is automatically taxed as a DE unless it files an S-Corporation election (Form 2553). If there are two or more owners of an LLC, it is automatically taxed as a Partnership unless it files a Form 2553. An LLC with two or more owners may file a Form 8832 with the IRS to declare that it intends to be taxed as a Partnership but does not have to. Technically, the IRS does not recognize an LLC for tax purposes—it is the underlying election that matters to the taxing authorities.

An LLC affords its equity owners the ability to *migrate* between these four choices, though the best way to think about it is that one can migrate from the first choice (DE) to the fourth choice (S-Corporation) *as a one-way trip*. If you migrate over time from an LLC/DE with one owner, to an LLC/Partnership with two or more owners, and then to an LLC/C-Corporation that makes an S-Corporation election, you will probably need to retain your S-Corporation tax status from then on as there can be significant taxes/penalties to backtrack after the Business has grown substantially. There are a lot of rules and exceptions to additionally consider, but these are the important basics.

Since a Succession Plan depends on a relatively high level of profit dollars flowing to each owner pro rata through a Tax Conduit structure, the C-Corporation, as a permanent option, can be eliminated from consideration for most Professional Service owners choosing an LLC. That said, the remaining three choices are all viable options for a Professional Services Business. Inasmuch as we will cover entities that make an S-Corporation election in this Chapter, the remainder of this section will focus on an LLC that has two or more owners and elects taxation as a Partnership.

Starting on the ground floor, an LLC treated by the tax authorities as a DE is a one-owner entity structure—the IRS treats the owner as a sole proprietorship, albeit one with limited liability. This fits our working definition of a Practice. Initially, and often until next generation owners join the Business, many LLC's start out as a DE, though the next step with two or more owners is what really matters in a growing Business with a Succession Plan. Once there is a second owner, the tax election defaults from a DE to that of a Partnership, although the addition of the new owner is the time to make a considered election of your preferred tax classification, which at this writing is accomplished by filing form 8832 (additional details provided on such documentation requirements in Chapter Five).

An LLC taxed as a Partnership is a unique entity choice affording the widest range of flexibility to a growing, changing Business, especially over several generations and perhaps in a regulated profession. For example, an LLC/Partnership can accommodate multiple classes of Equity should the ownership team ever need that option, and it can utilize virtually any type of Synthetic Equity plan imaginable, subject matter covered in Chapter Nine. Partnership law also allows owners to allocate profits and losses based upon criteria other than ownership percentage, and it may eliminate or reduce state-mandated record-keeping requirements imposed on corporations, such as annual meetings and minutes.

An LLC/Partnership offers a distinct advantage over all the other entity structuring options in that it allows for the exchange of an incoming owner's Book (cash flow, client relationships, goodwill) for Equity in the LLC/Partnership in a tax-neutral manner, which permits the Business to "onboard" or merge in next generation talent. This is a powerful growth and talent acquisition/retention tool. Onboarding talent (covered in detail in Section 4 of this Chapter) with ownership experience and a Book to contribute, completely resets the table in the world of Succession Planning. It is something that every small business owner and especially a PSP should consider seriously as a current and future option.

So what is the bad news? There are a couple of issues to be aware of. An LLC/Partnership, unlike an LLC/S-Corporation or even a basic S-Corporation, cannot treat an owner as a W2 employee, and it cannot offer tax savings on the payment of profit distribution dollars (from Basket No. 3). As a former owner of an LLC/Partnership, I can also attest that this is the most complicated entity structure on the planet, or at least it is on the shortlist. Partnership tax law is voluminous and written in many shades of gray. What that means is that you may need a more experienced accountant or CPA (and potentially even a tax attorney) who has experience providing guidance to Professional Service Businesses with the same entity and tax structure you have chosen. In sum, an LLC/Partnership is powerful, flexible, and complicated—though sophisticated may be a better word.

SECTION 3: THE BENEFITS OF AN S-CORPORATION

An entity electing to be taxed as an S-Corporation can be a smart choice for many Professional Service Practices that want to grow into a Business in support of a Succession Plan. Most small business owners, as well as their attorneys and accountants, consider an entity taxed as an S-Corporation to be the simplest entity structure to understand and operate—a real benefit if you'd rather work on delivering your chosen professional service. An entity taxed as an **S-Corporation** offers these benefits:

- Shareholders can receive treatment as W2 employees of the Business

- A shareholder receives their pro rata share of profits/losses and stock appreciation as a matter of law, not as a matter of choice as in an LLC/Partnership

- S-Corporations escape the double-taxation of a C-Corporation and, in most states, profits flow through to owners at a lower tax rate than wages (a self-employment tax savings)

- Limited liability in certain respects

- Unlimited life—for an S-Corporation with multiple

owners, it will continue to exist after the death, withdrawal or departure of any one of the owners

- A tax-conduit or flow-through structure

G2/G3, if the Business you are invited to become an owner of is set up this way, know that this structure will fully support a professional services Succession Plan.

An S-Corporation must meet and maintain certain requirements throughout the entire tax year (typically the calendar year) in order to qualify for the benefits. Among these requirements are that the entity must be either a U.S. formed LLC or corporation, it cannot have more than 100 shareholders, it is limited to just one class of stock, it must distribute profits and losses pro rata to ownership, and all shareholders must be natural persons or qualified trusts, and U.S. citizens or legal residents of the U.S., residing in the U.S. If, for example, one of four shareholders who is a U.S. citizen becomes a resident of a foreign country, the Subchapter S election could terminate, potentially affecting all the shareholders.

One of the most important benefits of an S-Corporation or an LLC/S-Corporation can be the self-employment tax savings (Social Security and Medicare). It is possible, with guidance from your tax advisor, to reasonably divide the business proceeds after expenses are paid into FICA-taxable wages (subject to the many federal, state and local taxes tied to employment compensation and which may also include assessments for unemployment and workers compensation) and FICA-exempt profit distributions. In sum, an S-Corporation only pays wage-based taxes on compensation to its owners, and not on the remaining profits paid out to Equity owners as distributions.

An S-Corporation must pay a reasonable salary to a shareholder who may also be a W-2 employee. The profits that remain after deducting reasonable compensation and operating expenses is not subject to federal self-employment tax. Note that city, county, and state taxes can significantly affect the choice and use of an S-Corporation and erode any tax savings. This is an ever changing landscape. Guidance on this front should come from your local tax advisor before setting up or making an S-Corporation election.

Reasonable Compensation is the wage or salary that is paid to a business owner to perform services for the Business before receiving a profit distribution in an S-Corporation or an LLC/S-Corporation. In the simplest of terms, to be considered "reasonable" by the IRS (always in hindsight), the amount paid must be equivalent to what a similar business would pay someone else with similar qualifications and experience to perform the same or similar services. The IRS looks at many factors to determine if you or another owner was paid reasonable compensation if you're audited on this issue.

In sum, there are many good reasons to set up a Business as an LLC or a corporation electing to be taxed as an S-Corporation, or to be a next gen owner of such an entity. Younger owners of a minority interest often appreciate the pro rata requirements on their share of the profits and appreciating stock value. PSPs who prefer to work in the Business rather than on it will appreciate the clarity and simplicity of this entity structure.

There are a couple of drawbacks to be aware of, other than perhaps the Reasonable Compensation issue. First, once the founders have set up an entity and elect S-Corporation taxation and then contribute their Capital Assets, the entity will have an ascertainable and, perhaps, significant value; if not now, then in the future. Changing from an S-Corporation to an entity taxed as anything else (LLC/Partnership or LLC/DE or a Sole Proprietorship) can come with a tax bill on what the tax authorities often consider a liquidation event for the corporation. Second, as we will explore in depth in the next section, S-Corporations cannot easily or inexpensively **Onboard** next generation talent, which is the ability to trade a Book owner's clients, cash flow, and goodwill for stock via a Tax-Neutral Exchange. And third, all of an S-Corporations' shareholders must agree to strictly abide by the federal restrictions to retain the benefits of an S-Corporation election—carelessness or an oversight by any one individual can result in retroactive treatment as a C-Corporation.

SECTION 4: USING A HYBRID MODEL

In the previous two Sections, we explored and examined the benefits offered through an LLC/Partnership and, separately, the benefits offered through use of an S-Corporation or an LLC/S-Corporation. This Section focuses on the unique strategy of using an LLC/Partnership entity structure in conjunction with a series of satellite Member S-Corporations, or LLC/S-Corporations (see *Figure 13*).

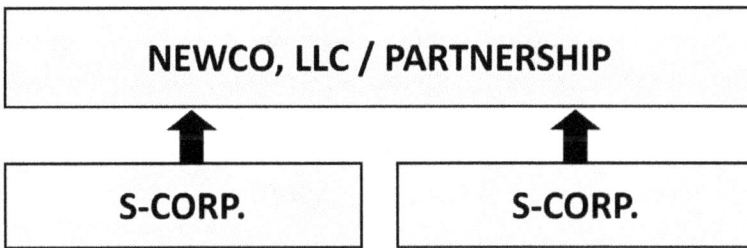

```
┌─────────────────────────────────────────────┐
│          NEWCO, LLC / PARTNERSHIP            │
└─────────────────────────────────────────────┘
          ▲                        ▲
┌──────────────────┐     ┌──────────────────┐
│     S-CORP.      │     │     S-CORP.      │
└──────────────────┘     └──────────────────┘
```

Figure 13

This combination provides the combined benefits of both entities to the owners of a single Business while eliminating or mitigating the drawbacks of each. Professional Service Businesses benefit from the tax efficiencies offered by an S-Corporation, but the owners of that same Business may also want to reserve the future ability to Onboard Book owners into ownership in a tax-neutral manner. There is also the possibility of utilizing a second class of stock at a certain level of success or value in the future. This hybrid structure, or **Hybrid Model** is the only structure that can do it all.

The need for qualified, capable, ownership ready, next generation talent (G2s and G3s) to join an existing Practice or Business cannot be overstated—that's why I'm writing this book. One way to do this, of course, is to recruit, hire, train and promote the talent from within. The problem is that this process takes time and may result in frequent misfires, which can be expensive and time consuming. Another way, and the focus here, is to merge in talent who knows what it is like to be an owner, has a Book of clients already, and has demonstrated that they are willing to take the risks.

The mechanics at this point may start to sound familiar, and hopefully so. Once a good fit is established and Due Diligence is complete, a Book owner who wants to join an existing Business and its Successor Team contributes all the rights, title and interest in their clients including related cash flow and goodwill to Newco, LLC/Partnership. Newco then reciprocates and issues a certain amount of stock (from authorized but unissued shares) to the incoming contributor of roughly equal value to the contributed Capital Assets (valuations are commonly performed on both parties or both sides of the transaction immediately before such an event). This is the process that we call **Onboarding**, a shorthand term for a **Tax-Neutral Exchange (or TNE)** process under the IRC (see *Figure 14*).

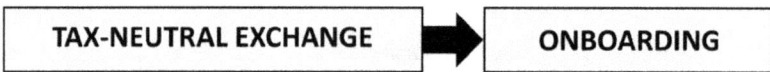

TAX-NEUTRAL EXCHANGE ➡	ONBOARDING

Figure 14

In fact, the most common type of "merger" between PSPs is the Tax-Neutral Exchange ("TNE") process. If the Business at issue is currently organized (or could reorganize) as an LLC taxed as a Partnership, **Internal Revenue Code (IRC) §721** allows for a TNE of assets (from the Book owner) for Equity (from the acquiring Business) rather than a formal, statutory merger. A Business in this setting is essentially acquiring a Book of clients and cash flow in exchange for newly issued equity and no cash. In effect, an informal merger of interests.

One of the unique traits of Partnership tax law is that this Onboarding maneuver can be done privately without having to file formal statutory merger documentation. LLC/Partnerships are uniquely well suited to do this, and it can be accomplished with multiple Book builders or new owners over the years. If this strategy is a serious consideration, then an LLC/Partnership, and/or use of this Hybrid Model, is the entity structure of choice.

In contrast, statutory mergers could be conducted under the rules of **IRC §368**, as well as applicable state statutes, if the Business is organized as an S-Corporation. The statutory merger process is more complicated, time-consuming, and expensive than a TNE. It generally requires that the sole proprietor Book owner first organize as an entity similar to the Business they want to merge into and then, after a waiting period, file Articles of Merger and/or a Plan of Merger that must be approved by the state in which each entity is organized or incorporated. If you go down this path, in order to avoid a step transaction, be sure to memorialize the independent business purpose that underlies the Book owner's decision to form a new company. Tax avoidance cannot or should not be the primary reason.

The Onboarding of a smaller Book or Practice owner into a larger Business with a strong, sustainable rate of growth and consistent profit distributions paid to the equity partners is an enticing proposition. It is the perfect set of answers as to why an individual Book builder, perhaps a G2 or G3 PSP, might give up *the going it alone route* and being in near total control of their own Book to become a smaller part of a larger team, and even to take on debt to buy additional Equity as part of a Succession Plan. If you are a Book owner in your late twenties to early forties, for example, and the geography works, you can Onboard directly into a G2 or G3 slot on the Business's Successor Team by exchanging your Capital Assets for Equity—if an LLC/Partnership entity structure is in place. Something to think about.

This Hybrid Entity structure is the most powerful and adaptive vehicle available to a Professional Services owner/ownership group, but it requires multiple entities to achieve these cumulative benefits, making this simultaneously the most complicated and sophisticated of the entity structuring options. This model also requires support from an experienced tax advisor and possibly a tax attorney to organize it all, but once in place, it offers the flexibility and Onboarding abilities of an LLC/Partnership with the W2 compensation and potential tax efficiencies of an S-Corporation. There is simply no other way to have all these benefits in one business structure.

SECTION 5: HOW STOCK IS BOUGHT, SOLD, OR REDEEMED

In any given Equity transaction between a G1 founder and a G2 or G3 prospective owner, there are actually three participants involved when viewed through the lens of a Business—the individual seller, the individual buyer, and the entity. Newco, LLC, the entity participant, presents numerous intriguing options and alternatives that every business owner should have at least a passing familiarity with.

In the Succession Plans that we are considering throughout the Chapters of this book, the basic rule is that *individuals* buy Equity and *individuals* sell Equity. In fact, this is how most Equity transactions occur. To be clear, Equity in this context refers to shares of stock that one owns in a Business, or Newco, in this case. But Newco, LLC, will also have its own shares of stock, properly termed as *authorized but unissued shares*. These shares don't count until and unless they are issued.

It is technically and legally possible to have a new owner (G2 or G3) buy stock directly from Newco, rather than G1 or any other individual owner, though this functionality rarely makes sense for a host of reasons. For starters, the payment for such Equity from G2 would flow into Newco's primary checking account where it can be disbursed as wages or profits at ordinary income tax rates (perhaps less in the case of an S-Corporation) rather than at LTCG rates, offset by any basis, as in the case of an individual seller. Newco certainly may have a need for such funds, for instance, to finance an acquisition, to repay company debt, to pay its bills or to enhance business liquidity. Those might be good reasons, but here's the catch.

Newco would issue *previously authorized but unissued* shares to the individual buyer, let's say for a 10% interest in the Business, putting more shares into play and effectively diluting everyone's ownership. In essence, G1, individually, will have sold no Equity and therefore will receive no money from the transaction (at least not directly), and yet is diluted and now, in simple terms, is a 90% owner, which affects their pro rata profit distributions and stock appreciation rights forever after.

In the right circumstances, such a transaction might arguably increase the value of the Business (due to having more cash on the Balance Sheet), but G1 is almost always more inclined to take payment in full as an individual seller at LTCG tax rates less any Basis, without any dilution occurring. If the Business needs the money, G1 can always lend it to the Business and receive interest on the loan. From G2's point of view, it really makes little difference who the seller is; you just have to do the math on the two approaches to see the benefits and detriments of these transactions. G2/G3, always start with the assumption that you will acquire Equity directly from a selling G1 owner.

It is also possible for G1 to sell their stock back to Newco in the final step of a Succession Plan, provided it is a valuable, profitable, growing Business with more than one owner and, preferably, more than one generation of ownership (though that still only takes two people!). Newco can buy, or redeem, a current owner's Equity, subject to statutory guardrails concerning solvency and liquidity issues. The legal term of art is a **Stock Redemption**. Newco then pays for the Equity out of its retained earnings, cash flow or with a bank loan (likely to be guaranteed by G1 in our working fact pattern). The Equity in such a transaction is effectively taken out of circulation and is now authorized but unissued stock. One way to think of this is *anti-dilution*. To better explain the details of these stock transactions, let's reset the table.

At the time Newco, LLC, is filed and initially set up, the supporting documentation should include some specific adjustments, or additions, to the typical LLC to accommodate the strategies involved in a Succession Plan:

1. Authorize 2,000,000 shares of voting stock (voting vs. non-voting stock is addressed in Chapter Six)

2. Issue 1,000,000 shares of that voting stock to the founders and any other immediate owners in exchange for their contributions of Capital Assets or cash

3. Install a Board of Directors (called a Manager-managed LLC in most states and also covered in Chapter Six)

4. Elect tax treatment as an LLC/S-Corporation or, if the TNE strategy is relevant, and LLC/Partnership

To clarify a couple of key points before proceeding, 2,000,000 shares are authorized and half of that, 1,000,000 shares, are issued, leaving 1,000,000 shares authorized but unissued—these terms (issued and unissued) really matter as we work through the concepts of this process. The reason for authorizing and issuing 1,000,000 shares of stock upon setup (as opposed to 100 shares or 1,000 shares) is to reduce the price per share to single or double digits so that in the first Tranche or two, at least, shares can be bought, sold or exchanged with greater precision (i.e., no fractional interests). Technically, an LLC/Partnership can create additional shares easily at any time but from a learning perspective, we will keep applying those corporate attributes and master the basic concepts first.

With these specifics in mind, let's get back to the stock redemption process so you can determine if this tool makes sense for you and or the Business you might want to be an owner of. When G1 begins the first Tranche of the Succession Plan and they sell 100,000 shares of their Equity Interest to G2, for example, G1's Equity Interest decreases to 900,000 shares and G2's Equity Interest increases from zero to 100,000 shares. G2 obtains a conventional bank loan to pay for the stock. Note that we still have the same 1,000,000 shares authorized and issued, or outstanding, in a single-class structure. And we still have the original 1,000,000 shares of authorized but unissued stock for potential future transactions or exchanges, *sitting on the shelf*, so to speak. This is a common first step, or Tranche, in a Succession Plan.

Now let's add a stock redemption event to the fact pattern. Newco is the buyer. Let us make this transaction subsequent to G1's sale of stock to G2 in the preceding paragraph by ten years and assume that two more next generation owners have also acquired Equity in the meantime. The current ownership structure, ten years down the road, is 60%/20%/10%/10%, G1/G2(A)/G2(B)/G3 respectively, with 1,000,000 shares authorized and issued to the four owners. For whatever reason, G1 suddenly wants to fully retire and cash out their remaining Equity. To do this via Stock Redemption, Newco acquires all of G1's 600,000 shares and returns those shares to the category of "authorized but unissued," putting them *back on the shelf* as well.

Newco now has 400,000 shares issued, all held by the G2 and G3 owners, with Newco holding 1,600,000 shares of now unissued stock (unissued shares have no impact on share value). The new owner-ship structure is now 0%/50%/25%/25%, G1/G2(A)/G2(B)/G3, respectively. G2(A), in our example, now owns 200,000 shares out of 400,000 shares authorized and issued, G2(B) owns 100,000 shares out of 400,000 shares authorized and issued, and so on. Each of the next gen owners are proportionally anti-diluted.

The foregoing example is offered to help you understand the basic mechanics of how stock is bought, sold or redeemed, and to highlight some of the less obvious ramifications. G1's sudden desire to cash out and retire will probably trigger the terms of a Buy-Sell Agreement and that may result in a discount to G1's sale price. The sudden nature of the event may also mean that Newco is the financially strongest and most capable buyer, especially if any of the G2s or G3 recently bought and financed their Equity. In addition and in contrast to all three of the next gen owners buying Equity from G1 upon their retirement, it takes only one transaction via a Stock Redemption to change the ownership positions of four individuals. Of course, the G2s will re-ceive a substantial increase in their share of any profit distributions and stock appreciation, and place the entirety of the debt obligation on Newco's Balance Sheet, perhaps all good reasons to consider this maneuver. To be clear, the use of Stock Redemption can be the right tool to do the job; it is by no means an anomaly in the world of suc-cession planning. But there is more to consider here.

For one, Newco's payment of FMV (perhaps with a discount) to G1 for the redemption and purchase of their 600,000 shares is not tax deductible to the Buyer; there is no Cost Basis accrued. This creates Phantom Income to the remaining owners pro rata who will pay taxes on money they don't receive (i.e., the earned and taxed income which will be used to retire the debt and/or pay off G1). The Successor Team members all become larger owners of Newco, without writing any individual checks, but there is still a cost to consider. If Newco was required to obtain bank financing, each of the G2s will probably be required to personally guarantee Newco's Promissory Note. And the Successor Team members acquire no individual Basis even though they are responsible for servicing the bank loan or seller financed note through the Business's cash flow and are likely personally responsible for.

This section illustrates the interplay between the Business and its underlying entity structure, and the individual shareholders of that Business. Some of this might seem complicated and *a bridge too far*, but in my world, the steps we've explored happen every week.

SECTION 6: GRANTING AND GIFTING STOCK

G2/G3, let's just get to the point. My advice to every G1 that I've consulted with over the past 30 years has been simple and consistent on this point. Stock, or any form of Equity, in a valuable Professional Services Business should never be treated like a birthday present. It should not be given away for any reason.

This is not meant to dash the hopes and dreams of the next gen PSPs out there who feel underpaid and entitled to some Equity as a result. The truth is that closely held, restricted and regulated stock has as many continuing obligations as it does opportunities. And owners of Equity in the context of a Succession Plan will be actively involved in the long-term success and growth of the Business; this requires an investment mindset on your part, G2 and G3.

Before deciding if these are issues that you want to fight for, it helps to know how these benefits work. For starters, the terms **Granting** and **Gifting** as applied to Equity are very different issues. A grant of stock is synonymous with the granting of a cash bonus at year end for a job well done. A cash bonus, which most G2/G3 next gen prospects are familiar with, takes the form of a check or ACH payroll transfer and, of course, comes from Newco's checking account. As the money leaves Newco's checking account, it is deducted as an ordinary business expense. As it arrives in your hands or your bank account, it is usually on a W2 basis and taxed accordingly. A grant of stock, or a stock bonus as it is sometimes called, works the same way except that it has many additional qualifications and complications built in. The stock comes from Newco's "treasury account," or authorized but unissued shares.

Many PSPs, G1s and G2s and G3s alike, often use the term "sweat equity" as to somehow justify the grant because it has already been earned. The common thought is that "I'm giving this to them because they've earned it." Unfortunately, sweat equity is another term for compensation and that is exactly how the IRS and every state tax it to the recipient.

Understand that a stock grant is not an individual to individual transaction. In other words, G1 cannot grant you some of their stock, G2/G3. G1 can cause Newco to take authorized but unissued stock and bestow it on a worthy recipient, often a key employee, and/or a G2/G3 next gen PSP. As the previously unissued stock is now issued, its value (best determined by an appraisal) is generally deductible by Newco as an ordinary business expense. As that stock, or Equity, is received by a key employee and/or a G2/G3 PSP, a myriad of possibilities unfold and this is where stock grants become surprisingly complex. Technically, the value of the grant is taxed to the recipient on an ordinary income basis but it depends.

The value of the grant and its taxation depend on the issues of vesting, valuation, discounting, tax deferral, tax acceleration, the terms of the Buy-Sell Agreement (i.e., can the recipient cash in the Grant a month later?), voting rights, continuing employment, and governance, and that is the short list. Working with closely held, restricted stock means all the details have to be considered and memorialized and that involves a CPA and an attorney, and probably an appraiser. Stock can certainly be granted, but it has to be done properly and with professional guidance and there is always a tax consequence.

Gifting is quite different. Under the IRC, the IRS defines a gift as "proceeds from 'detached and disinterested generosity,' ... 'out of affection, respect, admiration, charity or like impulses." Established law is clear that this test or threshold cannot be met when an employer gifts stock to an employee. A gift, if and when it meets the IRC criteria, is not taxable to the recipient. Stock gifted by an owner (usually G1) to an employee, or a son or daughter who is an employee of the Business is a taxable event, effectively a grant with all the attendant rules and qualifications.

Estate plans that involve family members are yet a different situation and go well beyond the focus of this book. Gifting in the context of a family estate plan is possible with the help and guidance of professionals, but having participated in a handful of transactions, I can tell you that it is not easy or inexpensive. If interested, start by talking to your estate planning legal counsel and your tax counsel. You'll also need a formal appraisal to establish the value of the stock as of the date of the gift, for starters. It might make sense given your circumstances, but it is always on a case-by-case basis.

I'd like to conclude by telling you that grants and gifts typically aren't necessary to complete a Succession Plan, but that's not really fair to the handful of successful, more valuable Businesses, family or otherwise, in which it might be helpful and financially advantageous. I will concede on that point and try to offer some practical solutions with the remainder of this section. Small business owners can almost always find a way! Whether that way can withstand a formal IRS or state tax audit is a different issue.

When considering Granting or Gifting strategies, there is often a common, simpler, safer approach that Professional Service owners can use and it falls under the heading of *timing matters*. Once Newco, LLC, is filed and set up, with assets contributed into it, a bank account opened, an EIN obtained, all the rules change tax-wise. At this point going forward, Newco has an ascertainable value and share price. When Newco grants or gifts shares to a key employee or other individual, the general rule, as you have learned, is that the recipient is taxed at their ordinary income rates on the valued shares, treating it as a form of compensation unless there is an exception or exclusion in the IRC.

The key is this—*before* Newco is filed and fully set up, the rules are different. When setting up Newco, before any valued or valuable assets are contributed into the new entity, one can justifiably argue that the shares of stock in Newco are worthless as the business does not own any assets and has no operations. At this juncture, other prospective owners such as key employees, an associated Book builder, a son, a daughter, etc., with something to contribute (i.e., goodwill, a client list, a desk and a chair) can do so for a small but reasonable amount of Equity in Newco received in exchange for the contribution and likely avoid any compensation/tax issues.

I often teach this concept with a bit more color to make it more understandable and memorable. Picture this if you will - once a circus tent is set up and all the edges are staked down tight, the only way in is through the ticket line. There is a cost to enter. But if one is helping to set the circus tent up and is inside when the edges are secured, well, there is no need to buy a ticket and pay the entrance fee. You are already in the tent! I am quite certain an IRS agent would find a different way to describe the process, as would your CPA, but this is my experience under the watchful eyes of many accountants across the country. It can work with new entities or those not completely set up.

If you are intent on Granting or Gifting stock, this is the time, place, and method to do it—after obtaining the approval of your CPA or tax counsel to be sure. Tax avoidance can never be the sole reason for this maneuver. If there is a legitimate business reason and a logical, defendable purpose, this is a way to get the job done safely in most cases.

Lessons To Be Learned

- The use of a Limited Liability Company, or LLC, is a most popular choice among Professional Service owners because it can change its underlying tax election, or status, from that of a sole proprietorship, to a Partnership, to a C-Corporation, to an S-Corporation over time.

- While G2/G3 next gen buyers/investors will have little input as to the entity structure, it is still important to understand how the different entities function and how each might be utilized in building a valuable, profitable, investable and sustainable Business.

- There are often two or three good, workable entity choices in most cases, in most states, and for most Professional Service models who want to develop a Succession Plan. All are Tax Conduits or flow-through structures and most utilize only one-class of stock, or Equity.

- One of the unique aspects of an LLC taxed under Partnership tax law is that an Onboarding maneuver (i.e., a Tax-Neutral Exchange) can be done privately without having to file formal statutory merger documentation. This enables Book builders to exchange their Capital Assets for Equity in a Business.

- Gifting and Granting are quite different equity sharing strategies. Stock is rarely granted or gifted to next gen PSPs as part of a Succession Plan.

Defined Terms in the Order Presented in this Chapter

- Tax Conduit (or flow-through entity)

- Due Diligence

- Employer Identification Number (or EIN)

- LLC/DE (or a Limited Liability Company taxed as a Disregarded Entity)

- LLC/Partnership (or a Limited Liability Company taxed as a Partnership)

- LLC/S-Corporation (or a Limited Liability Company electing S-Corporation tax treatment)

- S-Corporation

- Reasonable Compensation

- Hybrid Model

- Onboard/Onboarding
- Tax-Neutral Exchange (or TNE)
- Internal Revenue Code (IRC)
- IRC §721

- IRC §368
- Stock Redemption
- Granting Stock
- Gifting Stock

CHAPTER FIVE:
BUSINESS VALUE AND
VALUATION

Here is what I wrote in the first book of this series to the founding owners, or G1s, on this subject matter:

Respectfully, for all you may know about business value and valuation approaches, the value of your business is not what you think. That is a universal truth I've observed first-hand over the past 30-plus years in the M&A space (unless your profession involves valuing businesses!). I like to say that half of the owners I've dealt with underestimate the value of what they've built, half overestimate their value, and each half thinks that the other half is applying the wrong rules and logic to the process.

So, basically every business owner has an opinion as to their business value, and every business owner is likely wrong as to the amount. G2, G3, that is where this Chapter begins.

SECTION 1: BUSINESS VALUATION BASICS

Most small business owners have some idea of what their Business or Practice is worth, though most estimates are based on relatively simple rules of thumb which look at just one of many variables and try to draw a useful conclusion. Frankly, I did that all the time in my own professional services business just to keep a sense of perspective—and most of the time, it made me feel good or at least informed without having to hire and pay an appraiser. At the same time, I would never be able to sell stock or obtain a bank loan using *my number* without a formal business appraisal and an objective opinion.

I get it, sometimes when you are out hiking, it pays to get out your GPS and let the satellites tell you exactly where you are; other times it is enough to look around and get your bearings in a simpler way. It depends on how mission critical it is that you know exactly where you are or to put it more bluntly, where someone else thinks you're at based on available data.

G2/G3, the only way to know what a Business is worth *for the specific purpose you have in mind* is to have it valued by a professionally qualified and objective appraiser. Everything else is just a guess. And there will be a difference of opinion between owner and appraiser, and investor and appraiser—count on it. And there will be a difference of opinion between an owner and a prospective next gen owner/ investor, even with an appraisal—count on that too. Like it or not, every owner, current and prospective, needs to know the facts and the valuation logic at some point as applies to what you are building or buying into. Objectivity, along with some practical spreadsheet modeling, is how you overcome the differences of opinion.

The first thing to know as a next gen PSP is that Professional Service Businesses don't have just one value, and there is no single valuation approach or method that can be applied to every situation or to every Business. Just like with your car, value depends on *the purpose* of the valuation. Are you valuing your car to sell it to a third-party? To trade it in? Are you donating it to charity? Are you liquidating the asset at or near the end of its useful life? Depending on the purpose, your car has many different values across a wide range, and the values can all be correct. Business valuations work the same way, especially when considering the difference between selling assets to an outside buyer (i.e., an Exit Plan) or when selling a non-controlling Equity Interest to a next generation owner/investor (i.e., as part of a Succession Plan).

Traditionally, there are three valuation approaches, and several predominant methods under each approach that are used to determine value depending on your specific purpose:

- **Income Approach**
  - Capitalization of Cash Flows
  - Discounted Cash Flow Method

- **Market Approach**
  - Guideline Transaction Method
  - Direct Market Data Method

- **Asset Approach**
  - Book Value
  - Adjusted Net Asset Value Method

In addition to these professional approaches and methods, moving over to the practical and simpler side, Books and even one-owner Practices (review Chapter One if the specific definitions are not clear) are often self-valued using a **Gross Revenue Multiple** or **GRM**, which is called a rule of thumb. One specific example of a GRM is valuing a Professional Services Book or Practice at 1.5 x T-12 (trailing twelve months) gross revenue. The Gross Revenue Multiple in this example is 1.5, and depending on your profession, GRM's might range from 0.80 up to 3.0 x T-12. With a bit of research, you should be able to find an applicable GRM for your specific Professional Services venue, or perhaps an applicable range of multiples. The best way to arrive at a semi-reliable GRM is to find several recently completed, similar transactions and simply do the math (the final, total sales price divided by the gross revenue)—if you can find the transaction details.

Back in my day, as an attorney with a small Practice, I sold for a GRM of 1.0 x T-12 using an earn-out arrangement. G2/G3, you would be wise, if agreeing to use a GRM to determine a buy in value, to use a **T-36** approach—you'll get a much clearer picture of a Book or Practice's performance over 36 months than just 12 months. A T-12 approach might make you a prisoner of the moment.

A GRM is often used on smaller cash flow streams, think $200,000 to $350,000/year or less, where the logic lies somewhere between, "How wrong can I be?!," and "I'm not paying someone $8,000 to tell me what I already know." Books and Practices normally do not sell or transfer their expenses and liabilities to an outside or third-party buyer; that and the lower revenue sometimes negates the need for an appraisal. Profits or profitability often are not the defining result for Books and small Practices. And even if you own a larger and more sophisticated Business and you just want to satisfy your curiosity, a GRM appropriate for your line of work may be good enough (though an earnings-based multiple is still probably more appropriate for a Business—covered in the next Section).

G2s and G3s, keep in mind that these arguments and counter arguments as to valuations often do not stop a founding owner from seizing the highest and simplest valuation result from the realm of choices! That does not make it right, and it certainly is not the only or best way to obtain "the number" that you're expected to pay for and invest in. As for the need to professionally appraise the Business you wish to buy into, your bank will, or should, back you up without fail in absolute terms on this issue. My goal here is to help you become a smart, well-informed buyer/investor.

To this end, if you want to acquire an entire Practice or Book (via an Exit Plan for the seller) and it grosses more than $200,000/year, and especially if you, as the buyer, need to obtain a bank loan to cash out the seller, a simple calculation must yield to a formal valuation performed by a qualified appraiser. Again, the lender will decide the issue for everyone involved. End of story.

G2/G3, if you are buying restricted stock and a minority interest in a regulated Professional Services Business from a founding owner as part of a Succession Plan, you absolutely need an objective, professional opinion of value, every time. Rules of thumb and multiples of anything won't cut it. Next section.

SECTION 2: FAIR MARKET VALUE

One of the common ways to value a Business within the context of a Succession Plan is to calculate its Fair Market Value (FMV)—a term or acronym you will see frequently throughout this book. FMV is defined by the American Society of Appraisers as *The amount at which a property would change hands between a willing buyer and a willing seller, neither being under any compulsion to buy or to sell, and both having reasonable knowledge of relevant facts.*

FMV is a standard of value, or the definition of value that is being measured by an appraiser. FMV aims to reflect the price that would be established in an open and competitive market. It is a widely accepted standard of value when buying or selling privately held business stock or Equity. But there are other standards of value to be aware of as well.

In the simplest of terms, **Synergistic Value** refers to the extra value created when two businesses merge or collaborate, surpassing the sum of their combined, individual values. **Intrinsic Value** refers to the actual value of a business's assets, calculated based on its underlying business fundamentals, independent of its market value. In essence, it is a long-term perspective on a company's value, focusing on its ability to generate cash flow over time. **Investment Value** reflects the value that an investor is willing to pay to obtain an asset or investment based on that buyer's subjective goals, beliefs, and criteria. It can be higher or lower than market value depending on the investor's unique circumstances and perspective. I've reduced tomes to a couple of short phrases here, but the take away is that FMV, the most commonly applied standard, may place a lower value on a business than when using one of these other standards.

It is important to know enough to ask when the Business you are interested in becoming an owner of is about to be valued, or the related entity documentation (i.e., Operating Agreement and/or Buy-Sell Agreement) you are reviewing specifies the standard of value to be relied upon. To this point, many Buy-Sell Agreements include the drafters' default instructions to an appraiser as to the standard of value, and the valuation method and approach to be applied in the event of a sale of Equity. Non-attorneys call it boilerplate, but these specific instructions significantly affect the future of all owners, younger and older. Read it carefully and ask the necessary questions.

With all this on the table, let's put business value and valuation into perspective. Think back to the Three-Basket Cash Flow System where we examined how a strong Business can bring as much as 25% (or more) of annual gross revenue to the profit line after all expenses and owners' compensation has been paid. Using $2,000,000 in gross revenue, this leaves $500,000 in actual profits, i.e., Basket No. 3 (see *Figure 15*).

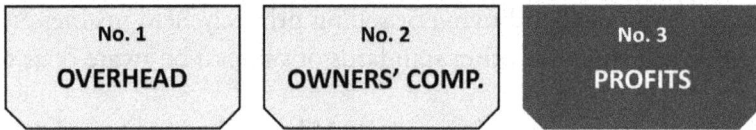

No. 1	No. 2	No. 3
OVERHEAD	**OWNERS' COMP.**	**PROFITS**

Figure 15

Starting here, let's talk about the conceptual valuation differences between a Succession Plan and an Exit Plan, because they are significant.

A Succession Plan typically requires next generation owners to purchase a non-controlling Equity Interest, using after-tax dollars, which by default includes the existing Profit & Loss Statement and the existing Balance Sheet. New owners, or G2s/G3s, are buying expenses and liabilities. For these reasons, among others, the profits of $500,000 earned from $2,000,000 in gross revenue, in this continuing example, are often valued in the range of 4 to 6 times profitability or **EBITDA (Earnings Before Interest, Taxes, Depreciation and Amortization)**, again using a simple, rule-of-thumb multiple of earnings for illustration purposes. That is a rough valuation for the entire Business in the range of $2,000,000 to $3,000,000 for many, but not all, Professional Service Businesses. Of course, the Business's specific profession, location, competition, niche, and growth rates also matter, a lot. Note that a formal valuation properly looks at dozens of factors rather than just one thing like earnings.

Let's compare and contrast the Succession Plan route to that of an Exit Plan, again using simple guidelines to make an important point clear. An Exit Plan often permits a stronger, larger buyer to avoid acquiring the Business's expenses and liabilities and, when structured correctly, the buyer can write off or depreciate the entire purchase price over time. These are some significant advantages over a younger G2 buyer/investor with little personal capital to invest. The result is that buyers or acquirers in a competitive acquisition setting often pay a multiple of earnings in an Exit Plan format of 7 to 9 times EBITDA, sometimes even higher in an organized market (but often closer to the 7x number than the 10x number).

You knew it was coming, but here is the caveat. These valuation ranges and rules of thumb are simply not reliable across the vast spectrum of Professional Service Business models and venues and locations. This is a learning exercise and the concepts are sound; but real numbers depend on specific facts and details and circumstances. The need to shift to a bottom-line mentality for value and valuation purposes, as a current or prospective Business owner or builder, is the other takeaway. G2/G3, if you're looking to acquire an Equity Interest in a Business, or to help convert a Practice into a Business, GRMs do not apply and are not helpful past a simple *smell test*.

So, one question that needs to be answered is why would G1 want to sell their Equity Interest to you, as a next gen PSP, for a 4x or 5x EBITDA multiple through a Succession Plan when they could sell at a 7x or 8x multiple through an Exit Plan? The answer starts with this formula, which you've now seen several times before, but this time with the emphasis on results derived over at least ten years, even as G1 gradually turns over the workload to their Successor Team:

WAGES + PROFIT DISTRIBUTIONS + EQUITY INCOME + STOCK APPRECIATION

A G1 owner who starts the Succession Planning process early enough can enjoy the cumulative benefits of wages, profits, equity income and stock appreciation, the accompanying tax efficiencies, even an expense account, all while reducing time in the office from Tranche-to-Tranche over ten to twenty years, maybe longer. Most founders (nine out of ten in my experience) find this approach, along with the control factor, to be more lucrative than selling for a lump sum to an outside buyer.

A few last thoughts. The level of profitability dictates Business value; those same profits are used to service the debt when G2 buys in. That is not a coincidence. Most Business owners do not have any experience with the appraisal process—selling Equity to you as a G2/G3 PSP will be the first time. And one more time - the only way to know what a Business is worth for the purpose you have in mind is to have it valued by a qualified, objective appraiser. Appraisers have their own rules to follow and they will tell you what they think and why.

SECTION 3: MINORITY DISCOUNTS / PRICE VS. VALUE

A **Minority Discount** is an adjustment to the FMV of an Equity Interest due to a lack of control, a lack of marketability, and/or a lack of liquidity. In a Succession Plan, G2 and G3 owners will invariably become minority owners for at least the initial Tranche or two, and possibly for the duration of the entire Plan. Application of a Minority Discount to the FMV of a G2's or G3's anticipated Equity Interest is a common and sometimes pointed discussion.

A **Minority Interest** is a non-controlling ownership interest, commonly defined as owning less than 50% of a Business's authorized and issued shares. A Minority Discount applied to such an ownership interest in a privately held business reflects the notion that such stock may be worth less than its pro rata or proportional share of the total Business value. Said another way, a G2's or G3's 10% share of the Business may be worth less than 10% of the FMV of the entire Business because that Minority Interest lacks control, is not marketable, and is not liquid.

The Fair Market Value of shares constituting a Minority Interest is not set or specifically established by any law or rule. The applicable range of discounts is generally between 10% to 40% percent with every situation being unique. It is appropriate to calculate separate discounts for a lack of control, a lack of marketability, and a lack of liquidity with the cumulative total to be within the general range of 10% to 40%. An appraiser will determine not only the FMV of the Business but also the appropriate Minority Discount to be applied.

A discount, if offered, should be applied fairly and evenly. For example, if a 10% interest in the Business is being sold to two members of a Successor Team (G2(A) and G2(B), for example) at or at about the same time, the same valuation method and the same level of discounting (if any) should apply to each Equity sale. This issue goes beyond fairness if the entity in use is an S-Corporation which is limited by law to a single class of Equity. Selling Equity at the same time to two different owners at different values could, arguably, create an issue for the S-Corporation owners and default them to C-Corporation status.

Practically, however, an appraiser provides the answer and the logic as to Business value and a Financial Analyst who does the actual math on the transaction including after-tax costs and debt service amortization schedules based on anticipated growth and profitability, helps to figure out the price. This serves to introduce the all-important concept of **Price vs. Value**. As a general rule, at least in a Professional Services Business, price tends to lag value, especially in T1, and this has nothing to do with the different EBITDA multiples explored in the preceding Section for a Succession Plan vs. an Exit Plan. In other words, the price of an Equity Interest in T1 is often effectively discounted from FMV to make the math work, a problem that solves itself with growth, adequate profitability, and additional Equity purchases. In T1, a 40% discount is rare; a 0% discount is not. It depends on the math.

G2/G3, practically, here is what you need to understand. After T1 is substantially completed and if/when you buy in again, the FMV standard is typically applied and is determined without a discount or such a discount, if included by the appraiser, is ignored. Most of the Succession Plans I've consulted on over the years utilize only one minority discount, in T1, and then never again regardless of whether the second and maybe third Equity purchases result in a minority position (i.e., three consecutive 10% Equity purchases). The problem is that the G1 seller(s) will not continually sell at a discount. In other words, in most cases, price equals value.

Many next gen PSPs think they are automatically entitled to a minority discount. That is wrong. In fact, it is entirely G1's decision whether to offer a discount; there is no law or other requirement to do so. G2/G3, understand that the application of a discount is less an element of negotiation or a contest of wills than it is about making the math work for an after-tax buy in process by a younger, often financially impaired, but still welcomed buyer. Very quickly in the Succession Planning process, this issue moves from theoretical to practical. It has to work for everyone.

The counterpoint to a Minority Discount is a Control Premium, though generally this is not an issue in a Succession Plan with multiple owners on the Successor Team. The notion behind a **Control Premium** is that if a minority interest is worth less than FMV due to lack of control, liquidity or marketability, then as a minority owner acquires enough stock to become a majority owner (i.e., more than 50%), they should arguably pay a premium on the FMV on that purchase. It's a good argument but I've never seen it actually applied in the course of a Professional Services Succession Plan.

Though most founders do not want to discount the sales price of their Equity, a Minority Discount can actually be beneficial if a founder is trying to Grant or Gift Equity to a son or daughter, using the argument of a lack of control and a lack of marketability/liquidity to legally lower the price of the Equity Interest and help the related buyer/investor justifiably avoid some of the tax consequences. In this sense, it works for both sides of the transaction though it must still be approved by the accountants who will file the related tax return(s).

As you are no doubt discovering, though the calculation of a Minority Discount is a technical and detailed professional process, it also has a very practical side. In sum, most G1s don't overtly provide a

Minority Discount to a G2 or G3 prospective owner who wants to buy in because an appraiser opines that they should. G1s apply the discount during the spreadsheet modeling if and when it is necessary because a Financial Analyst demonstrates the need and G2/G3 prospective owners are not in a position to close the gap any other way. It simply comes down to the math and, bluntly in the words of a non-accountant, is an excuse for getting the numbers to work. If a discount isn't needed due to a given Business's strong growth and profitability, it isn't offered or provided. If it is needed, it might even take the form of very favorable Seller Financing.

Though it doesn't happen very often, a strong, fast-growing, profitable Business might support G1's position that price should *exceed* value! At the very least, this argument might be used to counteract the request for a Minority Discount. As a fellow or past G1 myself, that's how I'd handle it, if it made sense—absent an Analyst's admonition to the contrary. G2/G3, you've been warned.

SECTION 4: RETHINKING COMPENSATION FROM A VALUATION PERSPECTIVE

Basket No. 2 in the Three-Basket Cash Flow System, as you may have guessed by now, is the variable. Overhead expenses can often be adjusted/reduced over time by a few percentage points, but for the most part it costs what it costs to run a growing Business. Maximizing Business profit levels still remains the primary goal for every Business owner because it supports business value. Business value, in turn, is the single, largest most valuable asset most Equity holders own, even pro rata—if it isn't, G2/G3, it likely will be in time with your help and support. Basket No. 2, figuratively speaking, sits in the middle and is what makes this new cash flow system all come together.

The point of this particular Section is to build on the initial Performance Ratios we established back in Chapter 2, Section 3 (*Where Does the Money Come From to Buy In?*) where we left off aiming for 40%/30%/30% ratios by stabilizing Basket No. 2 dollars in a growing Business. Over time, we also improved on this general goal with long-term ratios of 30%/30%/40%. A quick aside–focus on the strategies in this Section and not on the specific numbers or levels of profitability as every Professional Services venue will be different.

Many small businesses and Professional Service owners utilize an S-Corporation entity structure that can reduce taxes on the dollars flowing through Basket No. 3, assuming at least Reasonable Compensation is paid through Basket No. 2. This leads to a natural tendency with relatively equal levels of ownership to *overweight* Basket No. 3 as the Business continues to grow and settles the allocations as to the first two cash flow Baskets. For example, I've observed that a number of valuable Professional Service models successfully implementing cash flow systems such as 30%/20%/50%, or 40%/20%/40%, over time, Basket Nos. 1, 2 and 3 respectively.

Purposely driving more money to the bottom line, or to profits on your Profit & Loss Statement is smart business, but it doesn't work well with an ownership structure of 80%/20%, G1 and G2/G3 cumulatively—it is hard to make the math work when new, next gen PSPs receive so little, relatively speaking, of the profits. This means that the strategies of unbalancing the three cash flow Baskets, or our Performance Ratios, in favor of high profitability tends to work best starting in T2 or even T3.

As we rethink ownership level compensation from a valuation perspective, let's apply some practical thinking to level set Basket No. 2, in favor of higher profitability. Practically and personally, I have found it to be advantageous to set aside enough money in Basket No. 2 to pay all of my personal bills (mortgage, groceries, cars, insurance, savings, wine cellar, etc.) except for my city, county, state, and federal level taxes. Maxing out your Social Security contributions may also be a consideration if you're so inclined. If there is more than one G1 owner, compare notes. Wages are not based on needs, they are based on what works best for the Business and its investors. The key is to look at one's total take home pay as a combination of wages and profit distributions and any associated tax efficiencies.

G2/G3, it is only fair to acknowledge that ramping up profitability by under weighting owners' compensation could make the Equity you want to acquire in the future more expensive. Let's talk about that. On this point, it is important to understand that even if a Business can increase the amount of money allocated to and paid out from Basket No. 3, it does not automatically increase the value of the Business at least beyond a certain point. Appraisers, lenders, and investors will re-evaluate a Business's cash flow numbers in light of industry norms, a function referred to as normalizing the cash flow. Normalizing a Business's cash flow to re-allocate *more appropriately* to the other two Baskets, in hindsight, is done to make sure the Business can actually be operated in a commercially reasonable and competitive manner.

One owner, for instance, might take a bare minimum salary to pass the IRC reasonableness requirement and work 75 hours a week to keep the overhead and staffing low as well, proudly operating a 35%/5%/60% cash flow system. Such efforts will usually not be rewarded in full by an investor, appraiser, or lender—something to watch for when performing your Due Diligence in Tranche One.

In most cases, profitability or EBITDA, in a high profitability model is capped at a high of around 50%, depending on the circumstances and the type of Professional Services venue you work in. If you're a veterinarian and struggle to achieve 10% profitability, suddenly doubling Basket No. 3 by halving Basket No. 2 may well be met with the same normalizing approach. But if you have the ability to take more profit dollars home at a lower tax rate, it may not matter. The takeaway here is that the Three-Basket Cash Flow System can work any way a single-owner wants; once G2/G3 owners come into the picture, the Performance Ratios must adjust to benefit the entire group of owners, a necessary step in building a valuable, investable, sustainable Business.

This section started with Basket No. 2 as the variable, so let's finish there. Basket no. 2 is what pays the bills at home and it's often spoken for which is why we cannot reduce G2/G3's incoming wages. Basket No. 3, for the most part, will be tasked with servicing the debt on G2's/G3's Equity purchases. I'd argue that it is stock appreciation that really builds wealth, as stock appreciates tax free until it is sold (at least under the current IRC); it just doesn't pay any bills in the meantime. Next gen investors, even or especially those who are current key employees, will require that G1 finds an appropriate and attractive balance in the Business's cash flow system in order to present a compelling and complete package in terms of Shareholder Value.

SECTION 5: BUSINESS DEBT AND ITS IMPACT ON VALUE

Most Professional Service Practices and Businesses have fairly clean Balance Sheets. Many founders and entrepreneurs are debt averse, though I would argue that debt used strategically can be an effective way to grow and strengthen a Business.

When there is business debt, the most common liabilities and debts we see include an open **Line of Credit (LOC)** with a substantial balance (i.e., $100,000+), loans to an existing shareholder, equipment loans, automobile purchases or leases, tax liabilities, pending or threatened litigation, refunds or warranty claims, an EIDL loan, an unforgiven PPP loan, debt from a recent acquisition of another Practice and, on occasion, the debt from buying out a previous owner via a Stock Redemption (where the entity is the buyer)–not all on one Balance Sheet, of course! Real estate debt, not that unusual, is often maintained in a separate but related company.

G2/G3, understanding any debt on the Balance Sheet, as well as the debt service terms, is a part of the Due Diligence process. You will also need to watch for debt that does not appear on the Balance Sheet but lies in the expense section of a Profit & Loss Statement, such as a personally owned automobile or a plane. Balance Sheet debt should be a contractual obligation by the entity, or Newco, LLC, with a legal contract that you can review. But sometimes small business owners assign business-related personal debt instruments to the entity without a formal Assignment Agreement being used. That might be OK for one-owner Practices; once investors come along, the books and records need to be more carefully and formally maintained.

Speaking to the next gen PSP audience, an open LOC with a balance is not at all unusual. It makes sense if used properly and wisely. On occasion, however, owners use the LOC to support an acquisition, to pay off more expensive debt, for personal use, or to buy out another owner's interest. Technically, these particular functions are not what a LOC is for. A Line of Credit is for short term ebbs and flows in the cash flow of a Business rather than a long-term, self-granted installment loan. To this end, banks can require that a LOC be "zeroed out" at the end of every year or at least once in a twelve-month cycle (which is a good practice regardless of the bank's preferences). Again, these issues are all a part of the Due Diligence process.

As a simple but accurate rule of thumb, debt on the Balance Sheet is deducted from the value of a Business dollar-for-dollar. From an appraiser's or banker's perspective, there are various kinds of debt and there is a difference between short-term, medium-term, and long-term debt. Regardless, if I were an investor, a G2 or a G3, I'd argue for a dollar-for-dollar reduction in value and not budge from that position because the debt service dollars will have a direct impact on the profitability of the Business and the actual profit dollars paid out from Basket No. 3.

Acquisition debt is an interesting case for several reasons and depending on your perspective as an investor (G2/G3) or a seller of Equity, as in G1's case. On the one hand, acquiring a list and group of clients, the related cash flow, perhaps some tangible assets, and goodwill makes the Business more valuable, and often sends the three-year growth rate, or three-year CAGR (Compound Annual Growth Rate) soaring. On the other hand, the debt on the Balance Sheet offsets much of the value of the acquisition in the near term. However, as the Business continues to grow and service the debt, and especially if 90% or more of the client base transitions and is retained for at least one year and any synergies emerge, value will eclipse the debt fairly quickly. Add in the tax depreciation benefits of an asset sale/purchase and the numbers look better, sooner, as well. It is not unusual to find acquisition debt on a Business Balance Sheet whether it originated there or was assigned to the entity by an individual owner/buyer.

Acquisition debt works differently when a Book owner seeks to merge into an existing Business, a concept we referred to earlier and throughout this book as Onboarding (through a Tax-Neutral Exchange). Applying the basic rule that debt offsets value dollar-for-dollar, most Onboarding owners choose to hold any debt personally (such as from a recent acquisition, an open LOC, a car lease, etc.) and to service that debt personally because this maximizes the value of the assets that they are contributing to the Business via a Contribution Agreement. The higher the value of the incoming assets, with no off-setting debt, the greater the amount of Equity the Book owner will receive in exchange. Equity brings with it a pro rata share of profit dollars and stock appreciation in the now larger, stronger Business, courtesy of the Onboarded clients, cash flow and goodwill, and the addition of another owner to help run the operation and contribute to future top-line growth, and with no associated debt. This is a great way to rapidly increase Business value.

Pause for a moment and consider what we just laid out in the preceding paragraph. A new, Onboarding Book owner is going to hold on to any Book related debt while contributing all of their Capital Assets into Newco for a minority ownership position. That is a significant risk to be sure. Why would a new, younger owner do that, acknowledging that it might be you as a next gen PSP? The common answers lie in the benefits of joining a larger, stronger, profitable Business and having the opportunity to acquire a larger ownership interest in the future, using the machinery of a growing Business (i.e., Basket No. 3) to service the debt. Strong profitability and sustainable growth, along with a formal Succession Plan, are what will attract Book owners to partake in the Onboarding process.

It is not unusual for the Consultant/Plan Designer, the Financial Analyst, the affected owners and their local accountants to all get on a planning call to go over the spreadsheet modeling on issues that involve debt. Debt matters, but if well-managed, it can make a Business stronger and more valuable in the long run.

SECTION 6: THE ROLE OF LIFE INSURANCE

In every Professional Services Business with two or more owners, a Buy-Sell Agreement needs to be put in place. A Buy-Sell Agreement provides the terms for how all owners sell their Equity at some point in time under less than optimum circumstances. Triggering events in a typical Buy-Sell Agreement include death, disability, and loss of licensure, among others.

One of the most important aspects of a Buy-Sell Agreement, when a triggering event occurs, is the funding mechanism. Where does the money come from to buy out the Equity of an owner who must suddenly leave the Business? And who is the buyer? Term life insurance is one of the most common and basic funding solutions.

The amount of insurance does not need to be equal to the value of the insured's Equity. In a fast-growing, valuable Business, that's not really practical for most small business owners. The point of the term life insurance policy isn't to completely extinguish the debt on a buy-out, it is more properly used to defray the cost of the Equity purchase. If there is a single G1 and a single G2 owner, for example, the two owners may well utilize a cross-purchase arrangement where each owner purchases and holds (as the beneficiary) the term policy on the other owner's life. Application of the insurance proceeds are dictated by the Buy-Sell Agreement.

In cases where there are three or more owners, it is often more common and practical to have the Business buy and pay for the life insurance policies on each of the owners. In such a case, the practice is to not deduct the premium costs, and naming the Business itself as the beneficiary of any life insurance proceeds. As a general rule, paying the premiums with post-tax dollars should make the death benefit tax free, while deducting the premium as an expense, by the company or the shareholder, likely makes the death benefit taxable. The proceeds of any triggered policy are then contractually handled through the Buy-Sell Agreement in which case the Business (Newco, LLC) redeems the exiting owner's shares in full, effectively retiring the deceased owner's shares and putting those shares back into the authorized but unissued category, leaving the surviving owners holding all the authorized and issued shares. In the event the life insurance proceeds are not sufficient to extinguish the debt, Newco could use cash reserves, Seller Financing, or even bank financing to fund the balance. The choice as to the funding mechanism is contractually agreed upon when the Buy-Sell Agreement is signed or amended.

A couple of brief caveats for next gen ownership prospects as you consider the role of life insurance in your Succession Plan, especially its impact on Business value:

1. On more than a few occasions, I have seen Professional Service owners (G1) obtain a massive insurance policy (well in excess of any appraised value or common sense metric), expense the premium costs through the Business, and then use the amount of insurance to set a corresponding fixed or stated value which is memorialized in the Buy-Sell Agreement. This works on paper, but the problem is that if G1 does not die and trigger the life insurance funding *and still leaves the Business*, the Business's cash flow may well be insufficient to service the debt on the stated and inflated value. Also, any bank lender, if bank financing is used or needed, will probably defer to a formal valuation prepared by a qualified appraiser as to the Business's Fair Market Value; the amount of the life insurance policy may hold little sway.

2. We occasionally run into a do-it-yourself Succession Plan that relies entirely on life insurance as the funding mechanism to pay for the Equity value relinquished by any owner. Literally, the death of an owner is the centerpiece of the Plan with the idea that the successors will have no debt and the departing owners will be paid in full in a lump sum. It is not unusual for founders to say, "I'm going to work until the day I die." This is that plan! Somehow, I have never understood why anyone would want to be part of a Succession Plan that requires them to die to realize their value. There are better ways, but life insurance certainly plays a role in

the process. Look for it and understand the opportunities and obligations.

3. G2/G3's, as you perform your Due Diligence and read the Buy-Sell Agreement for your Business, take some time to read up on a new U.S. Supreme Court decision that impacts Buy-Sell Agreements, insurance proceeds, and business valuation. In ***Connelly vs. US*, No. 23-146, 602 U.S. ____** (June 2024), the United States Supreme Court ruled that life insurance proceeds paid to a business can inflate the FMV of the business. This case provides a host of interesting requirements and opportunities for a well-informed business attorney, perhaps in concert with an estate planning attorney, to rework a business's Buy-Sell Agreement, especially as to the impact of insurance on the buy-out valuation. This is more of a G1 issue, but all owners are expected to sign off on the Buy-Sell Agreement terms.

A closing thought on life insurance. The purpose of using life insurance to fund or partially fund a Succession Plan and Buy-Sell Agreement is not financial security for your family, or G1's family; that is a separate policy. The purpose here is to protect the Business and all of its stakeholders—its employees, customers, and other owners, in addition to the value of one's Equity Interest.

I've had the privilege of working with some very talented and experienced life insurance specialists. These professionals can offer some intricate strategies and life insurance products to solve Buy-Sell Agreement issues in ways that most of us do not even know enough to ask about. This may provide an answer for you so don't let this Section, which is based on the most commonly used approaches by other PSPs, limit your thinking. Ask the questions, do the listening, and then make your decision. Life insurance should always be included in your Buy-Sell Agreement funding mechanism.

Lessons To Be Learned

- The first thing to know as a next gen PSP is that Professional Service Businesses don't have just one value, and there is no single valuation approach or method that can be universally applied.

- Fair Market Value (FMV) *is* widely accepted as the appropriate standard of value when buying or selling privately held business stock or Equity.

- A Minority Discount is an adjustment to the FMV of an Equity Interest in a Business due to a lack of control, a lack of marketability, and/or a lack of liquidity. It is appropriate to calculate separate discounts for a lack of control, a lack of marketability, and a lack of liquidity with the cumulative total to be within the general range of 10% to 40%.

- The FMV of shares constituting a Minority Interest is not set or specifically established by any law or rule. In T1, a 40% discount is rare; a 0% discount is not. It depends on the math.

- As a general rule, price tends to lag value in a Professional Services Business, especially in T1.

- As a rule of thumb, debt on a Balance Sheet is deducted from the value of a Business, dollar-for-dollar.

Defined Terms in the Order Presented in this Chapter

- Gross Revenue Multiple (or GRM)
- Trailing 36 months (or, T-36)
- Synergistic Value
- Intrinsic Value
- Investment Value
- EBITDA (or Earnings Before Interest, Taxes, Depreciation and Amortization)
- Minority Discount
- Minority Interest
- Price vs. Value
- Control Premium
- Line of Credit (or LOC)
- *Connelly vs. US*, No. 23-146, 602 U.S. ___ (June 2024)

CHAPTER SIX: CONTROL MECHANISMS (OR, *HAVING A SAY IN THE PROCESS*)

The process of Succession Planning is all about a gradual shift in ownership and control. G1, whether as an individual or a small group of founders, starts off with 100% of the Equity and control. Over the years, G1 will gradually sell that Equity to the G2 and G3 owners on the Successor Team—but the shift in control is much more uneven in terms of the timing and levels of authority. Control and business governance issues consistently arise and require resolution prior to any investment.

SECTION 1: THE LEVELS OF CONTROL

Each member of the Successor Team is responsible for purchasing Equity at or near Fair Market Value (FMV), securing a traditional bank loan or Seller Financing, while acquiring a Minority Interest. Let's think about that for a minute—G2s and G3s, you are expected to make what amounts to a lifetime, or at least a career-length investment or series of investments. You will pay for your stock after taxes, with interest, and work to make the Business more valuable which means that each succeeding purchase is going to be more expensive. And then G1 expects to outvote you on every issue in at least the first Tranche or two. So, how does this work?

As you've hopefully learned in this book, the answer lies in under-standing and utilizing the mechanics of the process to address both sides' concerns and needs. For the purpose of this discussion, consider a $2.5 million Professional Services LLC/S-Corporation with 2,000,000 authorized shares and 1,000,000 issued shares. As we begin this exploration, assume that Newco has ownership ratios of 70%/20%/10%, G1/G2(A)/G2(B) respectively. As a reminder, S-Corporations are limited to a single-class of stock, or Equity.

In most Professional Service Businesses, there are as many as four distinct levels of command and control that can be utilized and coor-dinated to protect owners' interests. Think of these as the levels, if not the levers, of control:

- Officers

- Directors

- Shareholders

- Key Employees

Cumulatively, this is all about Governance. **Business Governance** comprises the rules, practices, and processes for organizational man-agement and control. It provides a structure for ethical, sustainable decision making, holding decision-makers accountable and oversee-ing a Business's actions for the benefit of all stakeholders. That's the academic view. In this Chapter, let's start to explore how to build a practical and powerful governance structure that can work for a G2/G3 investor/next gen PSP. We will begin with the Officers of a Professional Services Business because Officers make most of the meaningful decisions.

As a prospective G2/G3 owner, the Business you are considering buying into may not have all or any formally titled Officers in place (i.e., CEO, COO, CFO) on day one of T1—this is part of the evo-lutionary process of growing and strengthening a Business over time. More details and specific lists of the "C-level suite" of top executives ("C" stands for *Chief*) along with their attendant duties and responsibilities are provided in the Section immediately following. Officers in a Professional Services Business are usually, but not always, shareholders as well. The take away here, however, is that it doesn't matter how much Equity you might own as a next gen Professional Service Provider (PSP). If your skills align well with one of the Officer titles and duties, and you're so inclined, volunteer clearly and loudly and then go earn the job! This is a great way to have a say in a Business.

To put the Officers' roles and responsibilities into better context with the other levels of control, understand that it is fairly unusual for a small, Professional Services Business to actually vote shares on an issue. In my own Professional Services Business with up to half a dozen owners and 60+ employees, we did not have a single shareholder vote in 25 years and I hear the same thing from the business clients I consult with. Frankly, there is no point if any one owner holds 51% or more of the Equity Interests. But daily decisions still have to be made.

A Director, also called a Manager in an LLC, who serves on the Board, is commonly a shareholder who owns and has made a significant investment in the Business. To be clear, Directors do not have to be owners; in fact, outsiders to the Business can play a significant role on the Board, though often in a limited or advisory capacity. G2/G3, here is why this lever of control matters to you. Each Director has *a single vote* on a designated list of key issues for approval, regardless of their ownership stake in the business - this equal voting structure is key. At around a 20% Equity Interest, as we'll discuss in a latter Section in this Chapter, next gen PSPs belong on the Board in a voting capacity.

Continuing to work through our list, Shareholders are, of course, the owners, but they are often also the Officers and the Directors. And that is why we are talking about the control mechanisms of a small business, a Professional Services Business specifically. Formal voting of shares isn't how most decisions are made or actions are taken.

Experienced, loyal key employees may be assigned one or more of the Officer roles as well. A CCO or a CMO are common examples of non-owner, non-Director, key employees who wield a significant amount of authority and who are instrumental in a Business's success. Even though key employees who are Officers have no votes as Shareholders or Directors, they have an enormous amount of influence over the Business and they all report to the CEO. All PSPs who are or will be owners at the G1, G2 or even G3 levels tend to focus on the amount of Equity as the ultimate lever of control; the business of control is actually much more intricate. Still, it is good to be the King (or Queen) and Equity brings with it a host of benefits so let's focus on that next after putting our control levers and the respective placeholders into context.

Pausing here for just a moment, as a G2/G3 next gen owner or prospective owner, understand that control flows downward, as illustrated, from the top (Shareholders) to the bottom (Key Employees). Meanwhile, accountability flows upward, with Officers accountable to the Board of Directors, and the Board of Directors accountable to the Shareholders (see *Figure 16*).

If control is an issue at the G1 level, and it frequently is, then the founder should hold on to 51% of the outstanding shares, or Equity, for as long as possible. That is really the starting point for most first generation senior owners, or G1s as the Business grows around them and the Succession Plan unfolds. In time, however, it is highly likely that everyone, G1 owners included, will own less than 50% of the outstanding Equity. It has been my experience that the best Businesses are those that have or work toward a flatter ownership structure with no one, single, dominant (51% or more) Shareholder. In this respect, not only does everyone have a voice and meaningful influence over the direction of the Business, buying out a senior owner becomes not only possible but probable. Such steps require strong, confident, and wise leadership to be sure.

The need for and application of these distinct levels of control starts to make more sense when the ownership structure evolves from the 70%/20%/10%, G1/G2(A)/G2(B) in our example to something

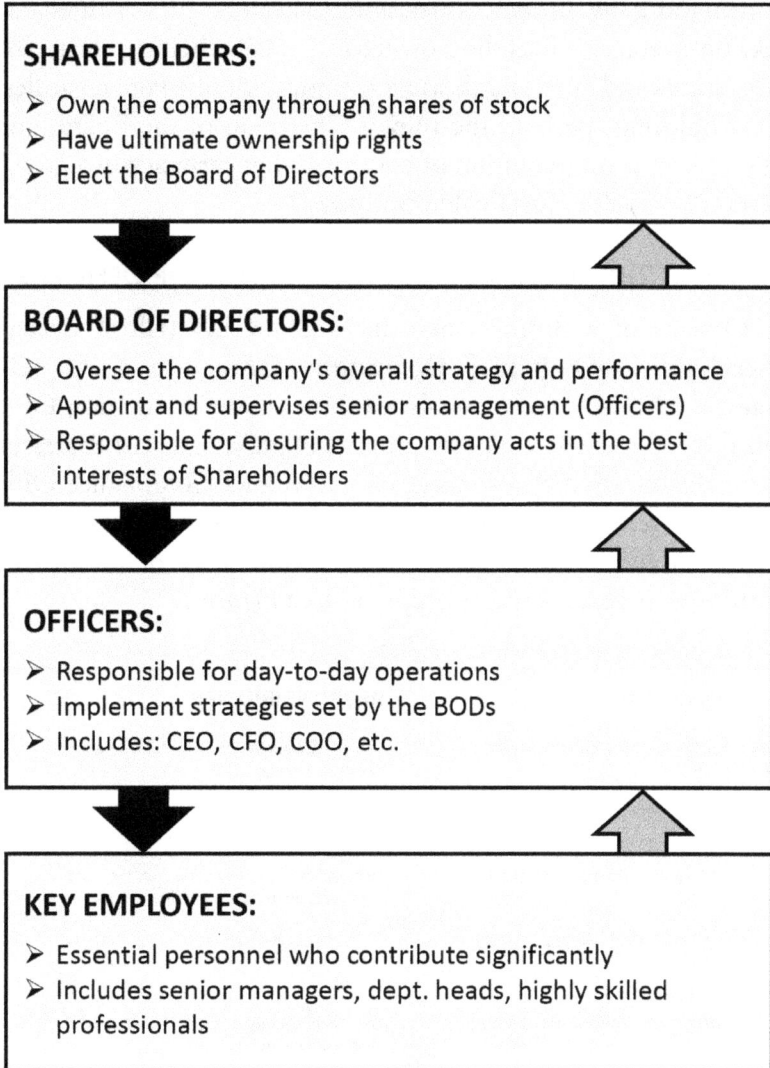

SHAREHOLDERS:
- ➢ Own the company through shares of stock
- ➢ Have ultimate ownership rights
- ➢ Elect the Board of Directors

BOARD OF DIRECTORS:
- ➢ Oversee the company's overall strategy and performance
- ➢ Appoint and supervises senior management (Officers)
- ➢ Responsible for ensuring the company acts in the best interests of Shareholders

OFFICERS:
- ➢ Responsible for day-to-day operations
- ➢ Implement strategies set by the BODs
- ➢ Includes: CEO, CFO, COO, etc.

KEY EMPLOYEES:
- ➢ Essential personnel who contribute significantly
- ➢ Includes senior managers, dept. heads, highly skilled professionals

Figure 16

like 30%/30%/20%/10%/10% among five owners and at least two generations of ownership, perhaps by T3. As the G1 ownership level starts to get older and begins to throttle-back in terms of time in the office and hours worked, the growth and profitability of the Business will demand daily, proficient decision makers. At two or three days a week, on average, a founding owner can retain their minority shareholder status and votes, a role as a Director with one vote regardless of Equity holdings, perhaps the role of Chairman of the Board, and… that's it. That is the evolution of control and governance in a growing, investable, valuable, sustainable Business.

SECTION 2: THE ROLES AND RESPONSIBILITIES OF OFFICERS

The Officers of a Business may include a **CEO (Chief Executive Officer)**, a **COO (Chief Operations Office)**, a **CFO (Chief Financial Officer)**, and possibly a CMO (Chief Marketing Officer) and a CIO (Chief Information Officer). Highly regulated Professional Service Businesses may also have a CCO (Chief Compliance Officer) on staff as well. At $5.0 million in gross annual revenue or so, it is time to seriously consider adding these formal levels of authority, one at a time, as necessary and appropriate (see *Figure 17*).

POSITION	RESPONSIBILITIES
CEO (Chief Executive Officer)	Overall leadership, strategic planning, and decision-making.
COO (Chief Operating Officer)	Oversees daily operations, including production, logistics, and customer service.
CFO (Chief Financial Officer)	Manages the company's finances, including budgeting, accounting, and financial reporting.
CMO (Chief Marketing Officer)	Develops and executes marketing strategies to promote the company's products or services.
CIO (Chief Information Officer)	Responsible for the company's technology infrastructure and IT strategy.
CCO (Chief Compliance Officer)	Ensures the company adheres to all relevant laws and regulations.

Figure 17

My advice is to include at least the primary Officer titles and a detailed list of their related duties and responsibilities in the body of the Business's initial Operating Agreement or Partnership Agreement, perhaps long before formally appointing and empowering each of these positions. Think of this step as shifting the culture from individual service providers to a coordinated team of Business builders and leaders. Understand that it is not unusual for these Officers to also be revenue producers and PSPs.

Here are the definitions we often use to start the process. These descriptors should be adapted to your situation, type of Professional Services delivered and your Business's needs and goals. But if I were a prospective G2/G3 investor, I would want to see these roles laid out clearly, in advance:

> **Chief Executive Officer (CEO).** The CEO is responsible for establishing the goals of the Business, providing for or guiding the development of the organizational mission and vision, growing the value of the Business and ensuring financial success, is responsible for capital allocation, and implementing strategies for meeting the Business's goals. The CEO shall meet with the other Officers to determine organizational policies and procedures, advise and present quarterly performance reports to the Board of Directors, oversee future planning for operations, encourage innovation and support a collaborative work environment, and analyze reports of the Business to proactively address issues, inform decisions and maintain overall effectiveness. The CEO may sign certificates for shares of the Business, deeds, mortgages, bonds, contracts, or other instruments, except when the signing and execution thereof have been expressly delegated by the Board of Directors or by this Operating Agreement to some other Officer or agent of the Business or is required by law to be otherwise signed or executed by some other Officer or in some other manner.

> **Chief Operating Officer (COO).** The COO is responsible for strategy implementation and management of daily operations. The COO is tasked with increasing profits and profitability, op-

erational efficiency, and quality control, shall promote workers to management positions, maintain or reduce service delivery costs, implement safety protocols, work with administrative staff to collect, manage, and distribute material information, and supervise and control all the assets of the Business; monitor the Business's budget and financial statements, and manage the daily affairs of the Business. The COO shall work with the CEO to align and achieve the Business's goals. In the event of the death of the CEO or their inability to act, the Chief Operating Officer shall perform the duties of the CEO, except as may be limited by resolution of the Board of Directors, with all the powers and subject to all the restrictions upon the CEO. In sum, the COO is a senior level executive who translates strategy into actionable steps, makes prompt and necessary adjustments to Business operations, and ensures that the Business's day-to-day operations run properly.

Chief Financial Officer (CFO). The CFO is responsible for and shall have charge and custody of and be responsible for all funds and securities of the Business, receive and give receipts for moneys due and payable to or by the Business from any source whatsoever, and deposit all such monies in the name of the Business in banks, trust companies, or other depositories selected in accordance with the provisions of the Operating Agreement, and in general perform all the duties incident to the office of Chief Financial Officer and such other duties as from time to time may be assigned to them by the CEO or by the Board of Directors. The CFO shall also be responsible for identifying and mitigating financial risks to the Business and shall manage relationships with lenders and provide them with accurate financial statements. If required by the Board of Directors, the Chief Financial Officer shall give a bond for the faithful discharge of their duties in such amount and with such surety or sureties as the Directors shall determine.

The overarching goals of developing this Officer-based structure, led by the Business's CEO, COO, and CFO, is to:

(a) Help owners understand that running a Business is about more than just revenue production

(b) Help each owner understand and respect what their partners are tasked with doing on a daily basis

(c) Provide support for future ownership compensation planning

(d) Provide clear information to the staff members as to which individuals are responsible for certain tasks

(e) Support a governance structure that is practical and skill-based, not centered on who is the oldest or the biggest producer or largest shareholder

Some businesses combine the roles of two Officer positions into one, energetic, fast-learning owner early on—as long as the work gets done, and it works for your Business, do it. Another possibility is to gradually assign a few of a specific Officer's duties to a key employee or a G2/G3 owner. If all goes well, and once most of the duties under a particular Officer's title are handled effectively, formally designate that person as the appropriate Officer.

Finally, notice all the duties and responsibilities that each Officer performs and consider how this impacts the governance, voting, and control of the Business itself. The daily work, tasks and decisions performed by the Officers as they fulfill their duties are not subject to a vote. G2/G3, if you are a hands-on kind of owner, you should aspire to being an Officer. In fact, if I were going to make a significant investment in a Professional Services Business, I would address this issue at the same time.

SECTION 3: INSTALLING A BOARD OF DIRECTORS

Practically, small businesses need to move fairly quickly and efficiently to compete and to grow. Listening to everyone's ideas can be beneficial; making significant decisions and moving the best ideas forward effectively is quite another. In this vein, many founders choose to install a **Board or Directors**, often called the Managers in an LLC, to oversee more important decisions and to create a formal governance structure for the larger owners and more senior decision makers. This mechanism also provides for some creative problem solving on the issue of control and *having a say in the process* of running the Business.

Let's lay the foundation for this Section. Newco, LLC, taxed as either a Partnership or an S-Corporation is set up with a single class of Equity, and 1,000,000 shares are authorized and issued. Business value based on a recent appraisal is $2,100,000 (or $2.1M). Following Tranche One, or T1, the ownership structure is, in this example, 75%/20%/5%, G1/G2/G3, respectively. To enhance the picture, G1 is 61 years old and wants to work until age 70, G2 is 45 years old, and G3 is 28 years old.

To state the obvious, in any vote of shares, G1 wins! But that does not work very well for owners like G2 in this example. G2, who agreed with G1 on a buy-in price of $370,000 at the time of the Equity purchase, obtained a personal, ten-year amortized, conventional bank loan. G2 wants and needs some control over their significant investment and the Business building and growth processes to come. One possible solution is to make both G1 and G2 Directors on the Board for this small, Professional Services Business.

At the Director level, as we noted previously, voting is handled in a different way than voting shares of stock. In simplest terms, it is one vote per Director regardless of how much Equity each Director might own, now or in the future. In Newco's Operating Agreement, the Managers, or Directors as we'll call them using more familiar corporate terminology, are each empowered to vote on a set list of key decisions for the Business that often include the following:

- Selling the Business to an outside buyer
- Entering into a long-term office lease agreement
- Taking on a total or an annual debt obligation of greater than $(x)
- Adding a new owner

- Diluting ownership by *Onboarding* an owner (via a Tax-Neutral Exchange)
- Adding a second class of stock (and/or changing the entity structure)
- Merging into someone else's business
- Amending the list of key decisions reserved for Director approval

...and those are just for starters. Your list may well be much longer. On these specific issues, the two Directors in this brief case study each have one vote regardless of how much Equity they own. This means, of course, that they must reach a consensus to move forward on these key issues. Of course, this list can and should be adjusted over time as the Business evolves, providing both or all Directors agree. In sum, this governance provision ensures that partners act like partners and, for the most part, leave their stock certificates at home.

As a suggested guideline, new Directors are added to the Board if and when they own about 20% of the total authorized and issued stock or Equity of a Business. This is not a rule of law, but my experience suggests that it is a good guideline to follow. The 5% owner, in contrast in our example, has the ability to influence but not to control and will not be a Director unless and until they acquire and pay for a larger Equity Interest—a second purchase and a second loan. The 20% rule echoes the tendencies of banks and landlords to ask owners of 20% or more Equity to guarantee certain business obligations. The few pushbacks by G1 on this issue, as to a 20% G2 Directorship, occur when G1 agrees to Seller Finance the entire transaction and G2 pays nothing down and requires a long-term, sub-market interest loan, to make it work.

As a Business grows in value and size and its Succession Plan evolves, there are some additional tools to use when considering adding Director Nos. 3 and 4, for instance. In Newco's Operating Agreement, the Board can choose to have two different written lists of key decisions. On one list are the key decisions for which a consensus of all Directors is required. On a second list of less critical or impact-ful issues, two out of three or a majority of the Directors might be adequate, assuming the Board has more than two Directors in the future. The point is, it is a small business and with some imagination, the owners and Directors can set up a governance structure that serves the interests of all involved.

Finally, G2/G3, please think about the long-term functionality of the Board and the "one person, one vote" rule in the context of an evolving Succession Plan. In most Plans, it will be necessary and appropriate at some point for the G1 ownership level to individually or cumulatively sell their Equity and own less than 50%. By having a permanent seat on the Board, G1 can retire on-the-job or at their own pace, and still have a meaningful voice in the Business operations. I would argue that this governance feature empowers the founding generation to step down sooner and with greater confidence. In the case where there is more than one G1, a Board seat for each founder also makes it easier for two or three G1's to own unequal amounts of Equity while still having an equal voice in the governance of the Business. As a G2/G3 investor, you need to know what you are walking into!

SECTION 4: VOTING AND NON-VOTING STOCK

It is not unusual for G1's local legal counsel to recommend that they only sell non-voting stock to the Successor Team (G2s and G3s). From G1's perspective, this is good advice. This Section is about the problems with this strategy in the field.

Practically, this strategy is not focused on the first Tranche or two when G1 still is a majority owner. As a next gen owner on the Successor Team, you need to understand that this strategy is aimed more at the time when G1, individually or collectively, will own less than 50% of the authorized and issued stock and the Successor Team collectively owns the majority. The point is that the Successor Team's stock is all non-voting, so while you, as G2/G3 owners, cumulatively may receive the majority of the profits and stock appreciation benefits as investors, G1 retains all or most of the voting control, depending on the composition of a Board of Directors.

Even though the IRS says that non-voting stock is not, for that reason alone, a second class of stock, next generation investors, along with their legal and tax counsel, and often their lenders, feel like it is and argue accordingly. On occasion, the Business's attorney gets creative and issues an actual second class of stock with more differences than just voting rights, not unusual in an LLC/Partnership. In the two dozen times I've worked with succession planning clients and the non-voting stock path was followed, or actually attempted, the G2 prospective owners argued strenuously for a very large discount on the per-share price of the Equity they were considering buying—enough so that each deal either failed or G1 realized that there were other and better ways to retain control and obtain full Fair Market Value.

Control of a business matters a lot to almost every G1 I've ever worked with. I often counsel next gen owners, especially in the first Tranche, to remember that the ability to influence can be almost as important as the ability to exert some control. It is nice to have the ear of the boss/founder, but not to have their burdens of ownership and leadership. By the time you buy in again in Tranche 2 and perhaps obtain another personal, ten-year bank loan, non-voting stock just isn't acceptable any more. The problem is that non-voting stock is hard to get rid of once it is written into the business documentation.

My advice to all owners, current and prospective, is to only issue and buy voting stock. G1 can use other means to retain control if that continues to be a serious issue.

SECTION 5: DRAG-ALONG RIGHTS & TAG-ALONG RIGHTS

A **Drag-Along Right**, sometimes called a 'Come-Along' Right or 'Bring Along' Right, allows a majority shareholder (G1 for this purpose) who chooses to sell 100% of the issued and outstanding shares of a Business to a third-party buyer, to compel any and all minority shareholder(s) (G2s and G3s) to sell their shares in the Business on the same terms and at the same time. A **Tag-Along Right** is often thought of as the inverse of a Drag-Along Right as these provisions are used to protect minority shareholders. G2 and G3 owners, in the event the majority shareholder decides to sell their shares to an outside buyer, Tag-Along Rights allow you to participate in the sale on the same terms if you so choose—basically, you cannot be excluded.

Succession Planning strategy and documentation often includes these rights but in an interesting way. In Tranche One (T1), which typically sees a first time G2 buy-in for 10% to 20% of the Business's total authorized and issued Equity, Drag-Along and Tag-Along Rights are both commonly included in Newco's Operating Agreement or its Members Agreement (if a Buy-Sell Agreement if drafted separately from the Operating Agreement as it sometimes is). Bear in mind that in the early years of a Succession Plan, where T1 is used as a test phase, G1 might still retain ownership of 80% to 90% of the Equity, and might be the only Director on the Board. Frankly, no one is absolutely certain of the new partnership and its long-term viability in the first few years of T1. Accordingly, G1 tends to be cautious and to keep their options open.

In T2, however, we see the strategy start to shift, especially if there are two or more G2's and they cumulatively own 25% to 30% of the outstanding Equity in the Business, or more, regardless of remaining debt service. When the G1's/G2's and/or G3's cumulative Equity ratios reach 70%/30% or more in terms of next gen investment, the G2s/G3s typically insist on having the chance and even the responsibility to be the buyers in case G1 decides to depart earlier than expected or if a triggering event occurs under the Buy-Sell Agreement. A second buy-in and a second round of bank financing normally causes this shift in thinking and tends to empower the Successor Team, and rightfully so.

In the Succession Planning documentation process, we recommend that the Operating Agreement and the Members Agreement in an LLC be drafted as separate documents, just as they commonly are in a corporate setting. The Operating Agreement, like the Bylaws of a Corporation, are higher-level principles and governance provisions that really don't need to be, and shouldn't be, redrafted, amended, or renegotiated every year or two. The **Members Agreement** (or Buy-Sell Agreement) is different and will be amended more often as the Business grows and changes and as the Equity held by each generation of ownership increases or decreases. This is another instance of applying commonly understood corporate attributes to the Limited Liability Company structure. Corporations have been around a long, long time; LLC's, for all their advantages, not so much.

A first-time buyer of a 5% Equity Interest, for example, often does not request many, if any, changes to the Members Agreement; after that same buyer acquires another 15% of the outstanding Equity with a personally guaranteed bank loan, they will look at the Members Agreement very differently. The point is, Drag-Along Rights and Tag-Along Rights can and should be renegotiated to reflect these ever present changes in the Business without needlessly opening up the Operating Agreement language as well.

One of the negotiation points to be aware of in a Drag-Along Right is called the threshold level, which is used to set the percentage of shares or Equity needed to trigger the Right. This threshold is commonly around 60% to 75% of authorized and issued shares. Other issues commonly negotiated focus on notice and timing requirements since the affected party (that's you, G2/G3) needs sufficient time to determine the facts, figure out the best course of action, and probably obtain legal and tax counsel of their own. For context on these points, here is an example of the opening provisions of a Drag-Along Right:

> **Section 1.0.** If one or more Shareholder(s) who, individually or collectively, own at least 70.0% of the authorized and issued shares (the Shares) of the Business receives a bona fide offer from a third-party to purchase 100.0% of those Shares, then such Selling Shareholder(s) shall have the right to cause each Remaining Shareholder(s) to sell all of their Shares to the same third-party on the same terms offered to the Selling Shareholder(s).

> **Section 2.0.** If the Selling Shareholder(s) described in §1.0 elect to exercise their Drag-Along Rights under this §2.0, then they shall deliver a Drag-Along Notice to the Business and each Remaining Shareholder at least 30 days prior to the closing of such sale.

Practically, it is rare in the Professional Services space to see a Tag-

Along Right exercised because the majority shareholder(s) will normally secure the highest price by procuring a sale of <u>all</u> the outstanding shares of stock of the business, especially to a third-party. Unless that third-party buyer fashions a special deal to entice and reward the next generation owners, G2s and any G3s will cash out with G1 and then negotiate on their own with the third-party if they wish to continue their employment and involvement.

Drafting these rights is the domain of an experienced business attorney, especially one who oversees Professional Service Business M&A transactions.

SECTION 6: SHAREHOLDER AND DIRECTOR MEETINGS

Yes, G2/G3, attending more meetings can actually be useful! The advice and strategies explored in this Section can also help to address the issues of control and *having a say* in the process of running a Business.

In any relationship and organization, consistent, orderly communications are vital to success. In a fast growing, dynamic Professional Services Business, it can sometimes be especially difficult to find time for all the owners to talk as a group, uninterrupted for an hour or more. For this reason, I strongly recommend that a specific date and time be scheduled once per calendar quarter so that the Business owners and leaders can slow down, sit down, and meet as Shareholders and, separately, as Directors. Once per year in the first quarter (Q1), I would take the meeting off site for half to a full day and use it to plan for the coming year. G2/G3, you need to help G1 make this happen.

These meetings should be treated with a high level of formality, something that will naturally creep in to the picture when new, younger owners are buying in and learning their new roles. Agendas should be prepared and circulated in advance for input. Each meeting should result in notes or minutes being issued for review and approval and then these minutes kept as part of the corporate records. Each Officer should prepare a report and/or presentation to share with the others about their challenges, solutions, and plans. Common topics should include recent business performance, upcoming revenue and earnings goals, staffing issues and future needs, financial statements, and more. In at least one of the quarterly meetings every year, talk about ownership and the Business's succession planning strategy, and perhaps review the original pro forma spreadsheet models and talk about expectations over the next five years–this will help to eliminate surprises between the owners, past, present and future.

These meetings present an excellent opportunity to help next generation owners learn how to lead and run a Business alongside their peers. It is also a good place for more senior owners to observe general competence, interest, enthusiasm, and attitudes from meeting participants which often involves non-owner/key employee presentations of information and materials. Who shows up on time (i.e., five minutes early at a minimum)? Who shows up prepared? Who doesn't? Who comes up with the best ideas, or solutions? These meetings are often one big laboratory!

During the one off-site meeting every year, invite the Business's legal counsel and, separately, the Business's tax counsel in to make a report on issues pertinent to the Business in each of their domains. Obviously, tax planning and tax obligations will involve the CFO, bookkeeper, and CPA as well, making this one of the few times that the entire ownership team sits down, slows down, listens and thinks together about these issues.

Depending on the Business's growth rates, or lack thereof, plans for staffing and payroll should be addressed at least a year out if possible and practical. Staffing and payroll affect issues of general overhead, profitability, and scale. Performance Ratios should be reviewed and anticipated. During these meetings, the founding owner(s) should take every opportunity to listen and evaluate, not just to talk and control the room. G2 and G3, you have to quickly and seamlessly make the leap from being an employee to being an owner–that is like crossing an ocean, so start swimming. Better yet, buy a boat.

These quarterly meetings provide such a great opportunity to grow and improve, and to learn how to communicate and work with each other as owners, through various challenges and struggles, all with senior ownership present and helping as needed. Do not miss this opportunity even if you think you already have too many meetings.

Lessons To Be Learned

- Business Governance comprises the rules, practices, and processes for organizational management and control. It provides a structure for ethical, sustainable decision making, holding decision-makers accountable and overseeing a Business's actions for the benefit of all stakeholders.

- Each Director on the Board typically has *a single vote* on a designated list of key issues for approval, regardless of their ownership stake in the business, making the Board of Directors an integral part of a sound governance and control structure.

- Drag-Along Rights and Tag-Along Rights are common in a Succession Plan, but must yield to the realities of the Successor Team and business growth/evolution.

- In a Limited Liability Company, consider drafting the Operating Agreement and the Members Agreement (Buy-Sell provisions) as separate, stand-alone documents just as in a corporation.

- Once per year in the first quarter (Q1), schedule an off-site Shareholders meeting for half to a full day and use it to plan for the coming year.

Defined Terms in the Order Presented in this Chapter

- Business Governance
- Chief Executive Officer (or CEO)
- Chief Operating Officer (or COO)
- Chief Financial Officer (or CFO)

- Board of Directors (or Director, or BOD)
- Drag-Along Rights
- Tag-Along Rights
- Members Agreement

CHAPTER SEVEN: LEARNING TO BE A GOOD BUSINESS PARTNER

Being the majority owner of a Professional Services Business is hard, demanding work. Being one of the minority owners is even harder and more demanding. I know. I have been both. This Section is about how to successfully navigate the challenges you will face, G2/G3, and to one day pass along the many lessons you learn.

SECTION 1: BEING A GOOD STEWARD OF OWNERSHIP

G2/G3, as you are now well aware, a properly structured business can theoretically last forever, or certainly well beyond the founding owner's career. The concept of being a good steward of ownership is that founding owners can use their businesses to accomplish good and to take care of all its stakeholders—clients, owners, employees, and the surrounding community. From G1's point of view, this may be viewed as an opportunity, an obligation, something of little importance, or something to pursue later when the Business and its ownership ranks grow enough to properly develop the concept.

As an overarching philosophy, stewardship emphasizes that owning equity comes with responsibilities beyond, or at least in addition to, profit and value maximization. Going back to the basics and supporting the purposes of this book, being a good steward of ownership starts with documenting rules that tend to go further and be more proactive than those in a typical Buy-Sell Agreement.

Formal Stewardship Rules, for example, might include an agreed upon requirement that G1(s) cannot hold more than 50% of the Equity Interests in the Business at age 60, and no more than 25% of the Equity Interests by age 65, and must sell, or offer to sell, all of their Equity by age 70—adjust the numbers and ages for your situation. The idea is that making Equity or stock available at set, predetermined intervals helps to ensure that you, as next generation investors, can plan for and make the necessary Equity investments during your careers. These rules also help make certain that the Business does not have to deal with a single, large, majority shareholder of a valuable Business who suddenly and voluntarily elects to withdraw or retire, an issue not always explicitly or well-covered in a typical Buy-Sell Agreement.

Every owner, regardless of their age, wants to be able to sell their Equity Interest, someday, at current Fair Market Value (FMV), for cash, at long-term capital gains rates. Accordingly, being a good steward of ownership requires prospective sellers who want to sell Equity under these circumstances to adhere to certain, written, pre-established guidelines if they want their full expectations to be met.

Functionally, the Business owners (G1+G2+G3) can agree as a group that in order to meet a seller's reasonable expectations when selling Equity, there will be established and reasonable expectations in return from the remaining owners. A common requirement is that a seller (of any age) must give at least 24 months' notice to obtain their full benefits. In the event an owner leaves and wants to sell their equity on, for example, two weeks' notice, then the FMV of their Equity Interest may be discounted and payment terms may be applied through Seller Financing rather than a lump sum through bank financing. These Stewardship Rules are put in place to ensure the Business remains liquid and sustainable, and that the Business has time to address the loss of talent.

For a Business that is developing a formal Succession Plan, Stewardship Rules can work hand-in-hand with the process. Effectively, such Rules eliminate the wait-and-see approach in favor of a written plan complete with designated timeframes and sellers and buyers in support of a formal spreadsheet model (the Equity Blueprint). G1s who will be obligated to sell their Equity by a certain date may also be predisposed to work harder at growing the Business beforehand to increase the value of their Equity Interest before it is made available to next gen buyers.

In terms of community support, some Businesses like to set aside a small portion of the profits (Basket No. 3) and support a local cause or charity. Sometimes, the preference is to have all the owners and key employees volunteer a certain number of hours every year in support of a cause that aligns with the Business's goals and objectives. There really is no limit to the possibilities of using a Business to do good for others and it doesn't have to involve money.

These Stewardship Rules, along with all the Buy-Sell provisions, should be reviewed every couple of years by all the owners, especially as the Business grows in value and the owners of significant amounts of Equity get older. G2/G3, this is an issue to revisit in the Q1 Shareholder Meeting every year. Good rules of stewardship may even help the Business attract and retain ownership level talent in the future because Equity will be available to purchase.

SECTION 2: OVERCOMING G1'S OBJECTIONS

Founding owners consistently struggle with certain aspects of this process—not so much with a Succession Plan in general, but with some of the mechanics of the process and the changes that occur by having additional partners or owners. It is not personal, G2 and G3. Still, you need to be prepared. In no particular order, other than perhaps the frequency of the objections that I have heard from G1s over the years:

1. **Sharing the Books and Records:** As a part of every new, next generation owner's Due Diligence regarding their

prospective investment, a review of the Business's financial statements for the past three years is necessary, or at least strongly recommended. The problem that arises is that many small business and solo Practice owners use their cash flow stream as their own, personal *piggybank* where they write off a lot of sometimes *interesting* business-related expenses—no judgment intended as I did the same thing. These matters, and the full range of such expenses, are discussed only between the owner and their accountant and maybe a bookkeeper. Sharing or disclosing this information to key employees-turned-maybe-investors (G2/G3, you can still say "No" after Due Diligence is complete), along with the founding owner's annual salary and benefit package, is often a point of significant discomfort when first setting up an internal ownership plan; not that anything is amiss.

Our advice on this front is to apply and use the Three-Basket Cash Flow System, at least as part of your Due Diligence if not as an overall Business cash flow management strategy, to determine if the expense(s) in question should be categorized as a part of the Business's general overhead (Basket No. 1), or part of a specific owner's wage/compensation package (Basket no. 2). This issue often comes to life, and to resolution, during the pro forma spreadsheeting process.

In many cases, owners in a valuable, profitable, growing Business are (or should be) provided with an expense account as a part of their base compensation package. That is CEO level thinking, and quite possibly something new to the cash flow management process for an emerging Business structure. A monthly expense account starting at $1,000 to $2,500, depending on Business size and cash flow, allows *each owner* to use the Business to support their efforts and work-related expenses, no (or not many) questions asked. Categorizing an expense, for instance, under "Owner's Expense Account" on the P&L Statement looks better to a potential investor than "Spa treatments at Annual Conference," or "Tesla Model S payments." Any expenditures in excess of the expense account allowance are deducted from the owner's base compensation.

Of course, if the overhead expenses and/or owners' compensation costs are just too high, then changes must be discussed and gradually implemented. G2/G3, I reiterate an earlier observation: the arrival of new owners and investors, however challenging, can be incredibly beneficial for a Business and its founding owner(s). Sometimes that observation is best appreciated in hindsight.

2. **Next Generation Successors Have No Money:** This issue often feels like a blocking maneuver designed to keep G1 and G2/G3 from even talking about a next gen buy in; sometimes it is. Let's put this into perspective. Unlike third-party buyers who tend to be at least two to three times the size and value of a seller's Book or Practice, most of the Successor Team members do not have sufficient, liquid funds to pay cash for their Equity Interest, and most can only make a nominal down payment on the purchase, if that. But that is not the end of the story; it's closer to the beginning of the story.

The Successor Team members offer something else and something more. First, they offer G1 the opportunity to stay in control longer and to enjoy the benefits of Shareholder Value much longer. Second, the Successor Team of next generation owners brings the benefits of time, energy, and the ability to earn and invest money from their wages, profits and growing Equity value over a 20 to 30 year Succession Plan (from their perspective)–(perhaps revisit Chapter One, Section 2, *Appreciating the Value of Your Earning Power*, G2/G3). Third, growth is the key to making a Succession Plan work for all involved. Next generation owners have the motivation to make a real difference on this front and to help the Business value double, maybe twice or more, during their ownership journey. This growth engine is what effectively pays for their Equity Interest. And as the Business grows, smartly, it should produce more profit dollars and greater stock value, all to G1's primary benefit.

As the process unfolds, Successors should have plenty of money—once G2/G3 learn to harness the machinery and any tax efficiencies of the Business to get there. G2 and G3 will have to learn to think and act like owners and there is nothing like signing a personal promissory note with a 120 month amortization schedule to add a little *spring to one's step* early on Monday morning of the next work week!

To be fair, during the first half of the Succession Planning process (T1, and at least part of T2), the founding owner remains in control, does most (or much) of the ownership level work and worrying, and makes most of the money. By the second half of T2, and all of T3, maybe even T4, the tables start to turn. The Successor Team, led by the G2 and/ or G3 owner(s), gradually moves into a position of control. G2/G3, this assumes that you've earned it, paid for it and have grown into proven leaders. At some point, accept that you will be expected to do most of the work, with the founding owner still making most of the money as they will still likely be the single, largest shareholder. The Successor Team's reward comes later, and it should be substantial, if all the Plan's participants work together and take advantage of building on top of an existing Business.

3. **I'm Paying Myself with my Own Money (Because the Next Generation Successors Have No Money!):** To be certain, there is only one source of money sufficient to fuel the Succession Planning buy-in process, and that is the growing, profitable Business. To put a fine point on this issue, the common and more specific objection is that the profits shared with next generation owners would have been paid out and taken home by G1 level owners if they had not sold the Equity in the first place. In the old days, when G1 also Seller Financed the transaction at favorable rates, sellers didn't smile when making this objection.

Selling Equity to the G2s/G3s, and then giving them the profit dollars to pay for it, sometimes doesn't sit too well with the selling party as a buy-in strategy. And if G2/G3 doesn't carry their weight *after* buying in, I'd be inclined to agree with G1 on this point. But this book is directed at G2/G3 readers who need to address this powerful objection and move through it to make the Succession Plan work, or at least for it to begin. So, G2/G3, this is a chance to listen in as I tell you how I would handle it with G1s.

I'd start by counseling the G1 owner(s) to remember that they are not (or shouldn't be) granting stock or giving Equity away to anyone. G2/G3 is making an actual investment. G2/G3 is either going to sign a long-term, personally guaranteed promissory note as a non-controlling minority owner, and/or they are going to contribute all rights, title and interest in their Book to a Business that G1 is in almost total control of. Either way, that constitutes a substantial risk. I strongly suggest that the best way to look at this is that G1 needs to take a short-term risk too and invest in every member of the Successor Team; this is part of building a sustainable Business. A small business is not risk free, it never has been and it never will be, but this is a unique opportunity with a lot of upsides, over which G1 retains most of the control. Absent that, G1 should sell the business to a third-party buyer and retire, letting the new owner take the risks and all the upside, or let the Practice die.

I'd add to this argument that G2/G3 will eventually be responsible for revenue production and growth, and as the Tranche-by-Tranche process unfolds, the G2 and G3 owner(s) must pick up any slack as G1(s) slowly reduces their time in the office as they get older. At some point, certainly by T3, the cash flows of the Business relative to G1, become "someone else's money." And sometimes, for the first time, that is when this process makes all the sense in the world to the founding owner(s); kind of like saving for one's retirement, far into the future. It takes some time to see the actual results.

SECTION 3: WHAT TO EXPECT AS A NEW OWNER

One of the most enjoyable parts of the succession planning process for me is talking to G2/G3 prospects and owners, and sometimes even their spouses. For most next gen ownership prospects, unless you have built and owned a Book of your own, this is a first time ownership experience. During these conversations, some of the commonly asked questions are these:

- How do I get paid?
- When can I buy in again?
- Can my ownership be diluted?
- Where does the money come from?
- What happens if this doesn't work out?
- How much of a say will I have in the business?
- What are the tax implications of buying this Equity?
- Does our credit score matter going in? Or…will this debt affect our credit scores once we have invested?

But my favorite question is this: What more will be expected of me as an owner? That is a question that goes to the heart of the matter of learning to be a good next gen business partner.

What more will be expected of you?! "Everything" is my answer. The best of you; all of you. The same thing that you will expect of your new partners. Ownership is arguable a high-water mark for a young professional. You will be asked to add the terms "leader" and "thinker" to your skill sets…not immediate changes or an escalation in contributions, but gradually, over time, to take your work and skills to a higher level than you may have ever thought possible. G2/G3, you will be expected to carry on the business and your role as a PSP, respecting the foundation you are building on and contributing to. In time, you will be expected to improve on that foundation and to make it even better, while still showing respect for what the founders have shared with you.

I have often been asked by the founding generation, G1s, "How do I get my key employee(s), or my son or daughter, to learn to think like an owner?" I respond with something like, "That's like asking, how do I get you to understand the feeling of skydiving and falling through the air at 120 mph with the ground rushing up at you?!" The point is, you don't, and you can't, other than jumping out of a plane! That's how it is with ownership of a small business.

So, G2/G3, earn the opportunity to buy Equity in your business, and then make it happen. Experience first-hand the power of the opportunities in front of you and the weight of the obligations on your shoulders. Signing a ten-year amortized promissory note and waking up on Monday morning with 120 monthly payments still to pay is one way to learn to think like an owner! Another is to sit down in those quarterly shareholder meetings and talk and listen, and then think. In each of my new business ventures, I found myself thinking about the future and what I could do with it almost constantly. That level of passion will take you to new levels.

What to expect as a new, next gen owner? For all you may know about your craft as a PSP, owning Equity in a Business will be new. You will be paid or rewarded differently than you are used to, not necessarily in amount, but in terms of characteristics. You may receive a W2, or a K1. You will move from wages + benefits and maybe a bonus to the benefits of Shareholder Value:

WAGES + PROFIT DISTRIBUTIONS – DEBT SERVICE + STOCK APPRECIATION

Your tax filings and cash flows will change, G2/G3 readers. You will begin to work more closely with a CPA and a bookkeeper, and annual tax planning will be the new norm. To this end, you will start to be able to see *what's coming around the corner* in a business sense (issues that were out of sight and out of mind as an employee). The Profit

& Loss Statement and Balance Sheet will become important tools by which you manage your own personal financial statement and wealth building goals.

As I get older, I find that I repeat myself more, though only on really important issues! One of those is "how you get paid as an owner." Just in case you missed it, read too quickly, or forgot, here is one of the Important Notes from the early pages of this book that I feel the need to drill down on right now, hopefully with a bit more context from your perspective:

> References in this book to owners receiving *compensation* for their work, *being on the payroll, receiving a paycheck*, or a *Guaranteed Payment to Partner (GPP)* are to be loosely applied because it depends on the entity structure or structures. There is an old saying that "owners get paid last" and it is an old saying that is still around for a reason. As an owner, and regardless of your age, generation, or amount of equity, there are no guarantees that you will be paid for the work that you do—if the cash isn't in the bank—you and your fellow owners may come last on the list of a business's obligations. Welcome to learning to think like an owner!

Seriously, being paid as an owner has its benefits and rewards to be sure, but those occasional recessions or economic downshifts that no one sees coming may affect owners far more than employees. And even if you own Equity in an S-Corporation or an LLC/S-Corporation and are technically an employee, you still get paid last, sometimes most and sometimes least. To be sure, you get paid alongside the other owners, but owners take up the slack. This is, in part, what to expect as a new, next gen owner.

Connecting the dots between implementing Stewardship Rules before or during T1, along with regular shareholder and Director meetings will help to develop a road map into the future. G2/G3, how can you make a meaningful, measurable contribution? Where is your help and attention most needed? When will the next ownership opportunity arise? How fast is the Business growing and/or improving, or not? It is always best to know what the questions and issues are before figuring out the answers. The answers are best derived by including the thoughts of multiple owners and generations of ownership. G1 might not know the right answers, but they will quite likely have learned what the wrong answers are.

There is a significant difference between how most G1s, or founders, became owners and how most G2s and G3s will become owners and this will affect each generation's perspective on risk and sacrifice, and ownership expectations. Most founders of a Professional Services Business bootstrap their way to growth and prosperity. The business grows by reinvesting the cash it generates, as opposed to taking it home. Most founders do not take on hundreds of thousands of dollars in debt when starting their new ventures, though it might feel like that when taking into account a seven-year office lease, perhaps an equipment lease, payroll, and more. G1 will remember the days of not earning much of a paycheck, taking on an enormous risk and many obligations. These experiences will shape their expectations of you as a new G2/G3 owner.

Though the memories will start to fade, G1 did have total control during this process, probably from the very first day. As next generation owners in a Succession Plan, G2/G3, you will have to purchase and finance each step(s) into ownership with a formal series of promissory notes, with interest, after taxes. You won't have total control over the enterprise, perhaps ever. That is a very big commitment especially for a minority or non-controlling Equity Interest. And then you may well be asked to do it again (T2), and again (T3). In the end, each generation will think they did it the hard way. And each generation will be right. What matters is that each generation also has plenty of motivation to come in to work bright and early on Monday morning and figure out the future, together.

SECTION 4: FAMILY MEMBERS AS OWNERS – MAKING IT WORK

This is a difficult Section to write, from experience. I will, in turn, talk to you, G2/G3, as though you are the relative who aspires to ownership at a Business where you work with or for a parent, a grand-parent, an aunt or uncle or other relative. I will also talk to you as a non-family member, key employee, who is watching carefully how someone else's relative is becoming an owner. These are commonplace scenarios, both part of life and work, and still difficult if not handled exceptionally well.

Nepotism is the practice of favoring relatives or close friends, especially by giving them jobs or other advantages. There is a good reason many larger Businesses have **Non-Nepotism Rules** to prevent favoritism and discrimination in hiring and employment practices. To be honest and transparent in my advice, in the 65-person Professional Services Business I was an owner of, about one-third of the staff were relatives or close friends! Some days were *very interesting*. But it worked very well for us and I can tell you (mostly) how to make it work for you.

G2/G3, for starters, let's assume you are related to someone at the Business where you work and you've earned the right to be considered for ownership. I do not make this statement lightly and, in fact, I think you have to out-earn everyone else for this opportunity. I think you have to pay for it, too—on the same terms and price as everyone else. If you get or need some extra help to become an owner, the entire office will know and, well, it matters, especially in a small business. Some parent/owners will say, "I don't care. My business, my son or my daughter." But the other staff members will care and if/when the clients get wind of such favoritism, they will care too—everyone has their own story and workplace experience. A culture of continuity demands fairness and transparency.

G2/G3, as prospective owners of a Professional Services Business, look around and survey the landscape. If the opportunity presented to you is more of a Practice by definition, understand that founders can and sometimes do pivot very quickly as to their chosen successor and will clearly favor a family member for that role. Founders can often look at their lifetime of work and develop an emotional attachment to the work and to the clients and feel a need to protect everyone, including their family. If there is only the one owner and they have a child in the business or in the wings, this is always a possibility. Just be aware and make it a part of your Due Diligence.

G2/G3, let's consider the situation in which you have no relatives at the Business where you aspire to ownership, and you've earned the opportunity, but…you're not so sure the same is true about the founder's son, or daughter, or niece or nephew who is also being considered or who is already an owner. If the founder, or G1, wants their family to become the majority owner and is going to do everything possible to make that happen, you can either live with it or not invest or look for opportunities in a different Business. If you are not comfortable at the start, you probably won't be comfortable at the end. One of the best Plans I worked on had a father (G1) sell to two G2's equally; one was his son, the other his son's good friend. Ten years later, the Business had grown immensely and a third, unrelated owner bought in. It can work but transparency and honesty need to be the hallmark of the process and early on.

In the thirty years I have been working on succession plans, I have seen very few family businesses where only family members hold the keys to management and leadership. This tends to happen in smaller, Practice-like models rather than larger, stronger Businesses. For the most part, I see family-like businesses that have one or more family members involved but depend heavily on non-family members to ensure progress and prosperity. In the latter cases, I have seen the successful integration of a next generation family member with one or two non-family members. It can and does work well when handled professionally. If each owner, family member or not, has to buy in and pay full FMV, with a bank loan, the water seems to find its own level very naturally.

Pay particularly close attention to the Business's existing documentation during your Due Diligence—its Operating Agreement or Partnership Agreement, the Buy-Sell Agreement and such. There should be a clear and fair transfer mechanism when the founding owner and parent or relative leaves the Business. There should be no inheritance of G1's shares by their related G2 or G3 counterparts, nor even a right of first offer or preemption right. Any type of direct transaction between relatives means that non-family members will not be treated equally regardless of their skills and commitment—and that is not a Business that I would want to invest in.

G2/G3, this is why Due Diligence is so important. My legal mentor told me something that I still remember thirty-plus years later. Paraphrasing, the message was *Due Diligence doesn't begin when documents for a transaction are first drafted - it starts the day you go to work and it ends on retirement. Be optimistic and supportive, but also keep your eyes and ears open.* The best you can hope for is even-handedness and transparency, and then pass along these same virtues to the generation that follows you. The founder's son or daughter or other close relative may be the best person to take over, but that opportunity should be earned and not automatically granted, in my opinion.

SECTION 5: TAXES, TAXES, TAXES

One thing that will certainly change after you become an owner is the complexity and control of your state and federal tax filings. This will feel like a new world especially as a minority owner of an entity that may well be unfamiliar to you (i.e., an LLC taxed as a Partnership, an S-Corporation, or an LLC electing S-Corporation tax treatment). As a next generation owner, you may have little to no choice as to the entity structure, and still, you will need to be diplomatic, empathetic, and even a bit demanding on the tax front.

G2/G3, one possibility is that you will never prepare your own tax return filings again! For a Business with up to two or three owners, it is more likely than not that the Business's CPA will also handle G1's tax returns, or at least one of the G1's tax returns if there are multiple founders. G2/G3, you could have your own CPA, EA (Enrolled Agent), or LTC (Licensed Tax Consultant) if you prefer. But as the Business grows larger and the number of owners increases, the Business's tax counsel or CPA may well come to represent all the owners and the Business entity for sake of efficiency and accuracy. There simply is not time, in many cases, to involve the services of four or five different CPA's per tax year per Business. In most cases, the CPA and the Business will rely on one bookkeeper to organize the books and records in support of the tax filings.

Practically, Business tax filings, even for a Tax Conduit with mostly intangible assets, are growing more complex. And when one factors in city/county/state/federal filings and, on occasion, **State and Local Taxes (SALT)** in jurisdictions other than where the Business is located, the entire tax process for all the owners needs to be handled by one, well-qualified CPA or accounting firm. That has been my experience. The more owners in a Business, the more certain this advice becomes. I concede that having more accountants looking over a business's financial statements can be a good thing; be prepared to be on tax extension most years as the various opinions are coordinated and final decisions are vetted.

Depending on the entity you step into, G2/G3, you may be an owner and a W2 employee (as in the case of an LLC electing to be taxed as an S-Corporation, or a basic S-Corporation), or not (as in the case of an LLC taxed as a Partnership). This is one of the reasons why I recommend monthly wages for the work you do (Basket No. 2) and separate quarterly profit distribution checks (Basket No. 3). You will learn, with help from a good accountant and bookkeeper, how to coordinate the cash flows through these two cash flow baskets to minimize surprises on tax day. Either way, you will become acquainted with the concept of **Quarterly Estimated Tax Payments**. These payments are required for certain individuals and businesses in the U.S.—they are like pre-payments on your annual income tax liability in lieu of withholdings.

Generally, you are required to make estimated tax payments if you expect to owe $1,000 or more in taxes for the year and you are a partner in an LLC/Partnership, or an S-Corporation shareholder, for our purposes. Many states also require estimated tax payments. Every year, upon completion of your Business's tax filing, your accountant or the Business's accountant will prepare your personal return and provide you with a series of vouchers for your estimated tax payments at the state and federal levels.

Keep in mind that the Three Basket Cash Flow System covered in Chapter Two, Section 2, could result in allocating a substantial amount of a fast-growing revenue stream to Basket No. 3, or profits, for which there is no withholding, even if you are an owner and employee. Add to this the fact that in a fast growing Business, estimated tax payments are calculated on *last year's revenue*—so you will always be behind in taxes owed. Staying current on quarterly estimated tax payments is something that every new owner learns and learns quickly. In addition, I learned to always over-withhold on my W2 monthly wages as an owner (Basket No. 2), at least a little. It takes much of the surprise away on tax day and I never regretted taking this approach.

I have worked with a number of Professional Service owners who developed the habit of under withholding on their wages, depending on their quarterly profit distribution checks to pay their tax obligations when due. This works well until an event occurs, such as October 2008 when the Great Recession began, more or less. All of a sudden, these Professional Service Businesses stopped paying quarterly profit distributions for a couple of quarters. Still, the tax bills came due even after several quarterly estimated tax payments went unpaid. My advice is to stay ahead of your tax obligations, especially as a younger, minority owner. Life is different when you have total control over the cash flow and profit distributions; G2/G3, you won't be in that position for a long while. Having to ask the founders for an advance is not a good plan.

You will also come to understand the concept of **Phantom Income** which occurs when an owner has more income allocated than they actually received during a given tax year. Since partners are required to pay taxes on the income allocated to them, not the money they actually received, failing to anticipate and/or manage Phantom Income appropriately can cause significant tax issues for partners. Issues that contribute to this problem are non-expensed life insurance premiums on the lives of one or more of the owners, debt service, and Stock

Redemptions of an owner's Equity Interest. Close collaboration between your bookkeeper and accountant can help identify and flag upcoming issues for the owners. Business documentation, such as an Operating Agreement or a Partnership Agreement, should also address these tax and cash flow issues and provide support to each owner for such tax payments if possible and practical.

Part of the process of learning to be a good, next gen business owner is to address and resolve these kinds of issues in advance. The perfect place to bring them up—those quarterly Shareholder Meetings covered in Chapter Six.

SECTION 6: HELPING G1 LET GO GRADUALLY AND GRACEFULLY

Learning to be a good Business partner and a good leader, G2/G3, demands knowledge, experience, strength, vision...and empathy. I would ask you to start by understanding that, for G1, or the founding owner(s), letting go of the Business they have built is hard. And even though a Succession Plan results in a delayed or slowed retirement, as a purposeful choice, it does not change the fact that the Business G1 started will one day go on without them, and hopefully do even better.

Early in my business career, a CPA friend, and one of my original partners, told me that the art of building a great Business was learning how, as an owner, to make yourself irrelevant. At various times over the decades to follow, I ardently disagreed, then begrudgingly moved towards it as a point on the horizon, embraced it half-heartedly for a time and then, looking back, finally accepted that advice. This is part of building a valuable, investable, sustainable Business, I was properly taught. If what you've built cannot continue without any one owner, it is not an investable Business. These are facts in my world; letting go, however, is mostly about emotions.

Having made it over that retirement hill myself, or at least the letting go part, I offered this advice to G1 in the first book in this series. *Don't look back—look forward and find a new passion and a new place to channel your energies. Do not stay in the business beyond the point where you're not needed and wanted. As a good rule, start by looking back on your typical work weeks over the course of your journey. Let's assume that, for instance, during your 50s, you typically worked five, 8-hour days (acknowledging that entrepreneurs work a lot more hours in the early years than that), or so.*

When you start to consistently work, on average over a year, four 8-hour days a week taking into account vacations, sabbaticals, sick time, etc., reducing your office hours by 20% or so, then reducing your Equity Interest by the same amount, moving to an 80%/20%, G1/Successor Team ratio. When your work week declines to three, 8-hour days a week, reduce your Equity Interest by the same amount, moving to a 60%/40%, G1/Successor Team ratio, and so on. But when you get down to two days a week on average, or less, the Business and its new ownership team have to move on and do things their way as they have an investment to take care of. At two days per week on average or less, it's probably time to let go and get out of the way, bluntly speaking.

G2/G3, these guidelines work well, especially in the absence of G1 having any specifics to offer or to chart their course. You should also talk with your G1 owners about implementing Stewardship Rules very early in the process such as T1. If G1 does not initially embrace the notion, come back to it again, and again. As an investor, I would consider these rules to be an important part of the buy-in process and the investment risk you are taking and, if necessary, I would even more strenuously argue for them before investing in T2 if they aren't in place yet. In the long run, this will make the process simpler and more predictable.

The Section about using a Residual Equity strategy (in Chapter Two) might also have some effect on G1's actual last day and how G1 and G2/G3, together, can better handle the letting go part. With these strategies in mind, have a heart-to-heart talk with your significant other and your business partners, look over your written goals, the pro forma spreadsheet model, and adjust the Plan accordingly as a group. The earlier you talk about this, the better; the future is easier to manage and plan for than the present. There is always a way to slow down or to extend the process if need be, but there is still going to be a last day for everyone.

Good investors base their decisions on specifics. That is part of learning to be a good partner and a good leader. Being clear and being direct about your expectations isn't always easy, but it is always a part of the job of ownership.

SECTION 7: WHAT IF YOUR SUCCESSION PLAN FAILS (OR TRENDS IN THAT DIRECTION)?

It is fun, and relatively easy, to be an owner in a Business where everyone gets along and growth seems automatic; profits just flow like rainwater off the roof month after month, year after year. But that isn't real life.

Failure of your Plan, or the Plan you are participating in as a next gen owner, G2/G3, is a possibility, even if you done your level best. Succession Plans depend on a lot of people and favorable circumstances over a long period. Some parts of this process you can control, and some parts, you cannot.

Sometimes it helps to put the words on paper—not all small businesses succeed. Not all stock increases in value, indefinitely, no matter how hard everyone tries. Not all investments work out and some can result in a complete loss of the invested proceeds as even the biggest and strongest investment firms all consistently add to their fine print, as a matter of law. Not all key employees should be owners and sometimes you don't know that until it is too late. Succession Plans can help you build a more valuable, profitable, and sustainable business. They also can and do fail to work out.

As your guide through the Chapters of this book, it is probably clear by now that I am an unabashed optimist, and two paragraphs in a row about possible failure is about my limit. When first starting my own Business, I used to get up every morning at 6:00 am and before leaving the house, I always polished my shoes, meticulously, and told myself "This is going to be a great day!" As some of you may know from experience, the first couple of years of any new occupation (especially that of ownership) are punctuated by more than a few difficult days, and weeks, and sometimes with paychecks that are too few or too small while you work hard to scale the learning curve. G2/G3, hopefully you will avoid the startup process and join an existing, stable operation, but the journey from a Practice to a multi-generational Business can still be challenging.

While I fully believe in this succession planning and Business building process and most every owner's ability to make it a success if they are determined, it takes time. You will need a good team. It takes commitment from all involved for a decade or more. People change their minds over that much time. The words in this Section are not intended as a caveat to all the Chapters and words in this book, just more of a reminder that even the best laid plans may not work out. Let's build from there and stare failure in the eyes and force ourselves to talk about it and deal with it.

My experience is that when a group of owners are unsuccessful in putting together all the pieces of an internal Succession Plan, and next generation owners never actually become owners, the solution set lies in selling the business to an outside third party. Sometimes, G1 can utilize a synthetic equity option and reward non-owners on the sale of the business contractually, without having actual equity bought and sold between G1, G2/G3. Why would G1 do this? Because G1 gets to keep full control and, if the incentives are strong enough, retain and reward next generation key employees for helping them grow and strengthen the business and add value to the eventual sales price. As a potential G2, this is a good solution if the sale does not take too long to happen and everything is put in writing.

Another possibility is to proceed with the purchase and sale of Equity by one of more G2s/G3s and use a non-recourse note—a possibility especially when Seller Financing is offered. A **Non-Recourse Note** does not allow the lender, usually G1, to pursue anything other than the collateral, which is the stock in the transaction, on a default. For example, if a borrower defaults on a nonrecourse home loan, the lender can only foreclose on the home. The bank, or G1 in this example, generally cannot take further legal action to collect any money owed on the debt beyond the value of the collateral. Whether a debt is or can be nonrecourse may vary from state to state. Non-Recourse Notes, if and when used, tend to be a Tranche One device and only if Seller Financed, part of that *test phase* I alluded to earlier. It can take some pressure off of the initial buy-in process and give everyone time to see if it can really work.

G2/G3, if your Succession Plan is underway and you've bought in without a Non-Recourse Note, the Buy-Sell Agreement tends to be the go-to document for what comes next. Start there. The rules under a default (G2 or G3 stops paying or is unable to fulfill their obligations for whatever reason), with a **Full Recourse Loan**, can be brutal and expensive. Full Recourse means that even if the value of the property used as collateral for the loan, like a house, is less than the outstanding debt, you are still responsible for the remaining balance. The same logic applies if the value of your purchased Equity Interest depreciates over time. So, don't default. Before that happens, talk to your partner or partners and find a solution, even if the result is to put everyone back as closely as possible to where they were before the transaction took place.

It is wise to also consider, with the help of a good legal draftsperson, adding in some formulaic safeguards on the debt service in the event of a material downturn in a Business's revenue stream. Such provisions can be included or added to the Buy-Sell Agreement and/or a promissory note and may provide for a reduction in payments if the Business has been hindered in such a way that it is long term and, perhaps, permanent. One example is that growth or profits substantially fail to meet expectations, leaving the investors with no practical way to extinguish the debt. Banks don't care and that isn't their business model. Sellers who act as the bank (i.e., Seller Financing) will care and that matters in the early Tranches of a Succession Plan.

Succession Plans don't have winners and losers as part of the same team; everyone needs to win or at least work together towards that end. There is almost always a way to get this done, and certainly a better way than quitting unilaterally and incurring G1's wrath (and contractual rights). Good partners, like good marriages, require that the participants learn how to solve problems together, especially when things aren't going so well. That's life. That's business. If being a great next gen business partner were easy, everyone would do it!

Lessons To Be Learned

- Buy-Sell Agreements are often used to address owner withdrawals due to death, disability, and loss of licensure or a significant disciplinary event, even crimes of moral turpitude. Stewardship Rules can be used to fill in the gaps and address other issues—creating predictability and certainty.

- Stewardship Rules can be used to require an owner who wants to sell their Equity to adhere to certain, written, pre-established guidelines including adequate notice and/or a requirement to gradually reduce their Equity Interest at certain age points, making the Equity available for next gen owners to acquire.

- The Three-Basket Cash Flow System covered in Chapter Two, Section 2, can result in allocating a substantial amount of a growing revenue stream to Basket No. 3, or profits, the distribution of which is not subject to tax withholding. Quarterly estimated tax payments may not be sufficient to address an owner's tax liability, so utilizing the withholding function of W2 employment status, as an owner, can be beneficial with a good tax plan.

- Not all small businesses succeed. Not all stock increases in value, indefinitely, no matter how hard everyone tries. Not all investments work out. These are the realities of any and every investment in a Professional Services Business.

- A Non-Recourse Note does not allow the lender, usually G1, to pursue anything other than the collateral, which is the stock in the transaction, on a default.

- It is wise to also consider, with the help of a good legal draftsperson, adding in some formulaic safeguards on the debt service in the event of a material downturn in a Business's revenue stream.

Defined Terms in the Order Presented in this Chapter

- Stewardship Rules
- Nepotism
- Non-Nepotism Rules
- State and Local Taxes (or, SALT)

- Quarterly Estimated Tax Payments
- Phantom Income
- Non-Recourse Note
- Full Recourse Loan

CHAPTER EIGHT:
THE IMPORTANCE OF BUSINESS
GROWTH AND DEVELOPMENT

G2/G3 owners, one distinct possibility to consider is that your ownership opportunity will present itself before, perhaps well before, the foundations of a valuable, profitable, investable Business have been put in place. In other words, you only have a chance to buy Equity in a smaller, less developed Book or Practice (see Chapter One for the specific definitions of those terms). It may fall on you, at least in part, to help build that valuable, profitable growing Business. This is the part where opportunity shows up for breakfast dressed in work clothes!

SECTION 1: GROW, GROW, GROW!

Back in Chapter Two, we examined the issue of where the money comes from to pay for an Equity purchase. The answer, to refresh your memory, lies in high or higher levels of profitability (Basket No. 3) fueled by steady, strong top-line growth over time. Ideally, this growing revenue stream is accompanied by greater efficiencies, or scale, as well. This money trail flows into and supports either bank financing or seller financing, and it makes the Business more valuable over time. Growth is imperative.

The concept is relatively simple: multiple generations of motivated owners working together are capable of generating higher revenue growth over a longer period than a single, experienced but aging founder, or even a small group of similarly aged founding owners. It is the execution of the concept that is sometimes complex.

Top-line growth rates work well as a measure of success from one year to the next for small businesses and Professional Service owners. Even though much of our focus in building an Equity-Centric Business is on profitability, gross revenue numbers are important too. These results are typically available to all founders even from their days as sole proprietorships and tracking such revenue growth over increments of three to five years is highly informative to an owner (and investor). In this Section, the focus is on top-line growth, or gross revenue.

If a Business grows in terms of top-line gross revenue from $1,000,000 to $2,000,000 over a five-year period, that equates to a **CAGR (Compound Annual Growth Rate)** of 14.9%/year. Profits are still the ultimate measure of value and success, but they are not the only measurement tool an owner should rely on. The calculation process of a CAGR requires three inputs: (1) the beginning value, (2) the ending value, and (3) the period. A CAGR takes into account the effect of compounding which means that the growth builds upon itself. To calculate your CAGR over any period you choose, just use one of the many free and readily available online calculators built for this purpose.

Let's talk about why it matters, especially to an investing next gen owner. I met a gentleman midway through my career who owned a Professional Services Business in the field of wealth management and insurance. He led a successful team for over 40 years and, when he sold the last of his equity to his three G2s/G3s at age 75 and retired with an appraised business value just north of $25 million, he told me his simple philosophy that he frequently shared with his next gen owners: "If a small business doesn't grow by at least 15% a year, top line, it's dying." Take that for what it is worth. As a business owner, it became my North Star.

Growth is particularly important in the Succession Planning process, though it does not require a 15% CAGR into perpetuity to make the plan work. Strong, steady, profitable growth is the goal and predictability matters to those who are or will be investors. A simple and effective way to approach the growth process, and to set goals for the Business, is to calculate how long it will take to double in value, especially with help from additional owner(s) and perhaps some innovative thinking as a team.

The time to double in size is 70 divided by the constant annual growth rate you are targeting. This is about setting goals. For instance, consider an annual target growth rate of 10%. According to the **Rule of 70**, it will take 7 years (70/10) for the quantity to double. At an annual growth rate of 15%, your Business will double in value in just over four and a half years (70/15 = 4.67). The similar **Rule of 72** is considered more accurate for higher growth rates (typically 10% or more), and is easily divisible by more numbers. This is thinking about where your Business is going or where it needs to go. How it gets there is a different matter.

There is a common misperception by smaller Book builders and Practice owners (e.g., sub $1,000,000 in gross annual revenues) that a top-line growth rate of 10% to 15%, or more, is unsustainable as a Business grows larger. In other words, it is easier to grow faster year to year when you are a smaller Book or Practice. Having been there and done that, I would argue the opposite. In fact, as a Business gets larger it can and should develop a stronger and deeper bench of talent—people you couldn't afford or even attract as a Practice owner. A Business has the ability, for example, to invest specifically in marketing and sales professionals and not fully tasking individual owners and PSPs to be the primary revenue generators.

As a result, with growth, the Business's leadership should have the funds to hire key staff members who *actually have education, skills, and experience* in marketing a Professional Services Business in your specific venue. A larger Business, armed with a budget and clear, specific growth, marketing, and sales goals to achieve as a group is arguably much better positioned to consistently grow at higher levels and for longer periods of time than a smaller Practice that depends on singular, uncoordinated efforts. That has been my experience over the past 30 years.

I recognize that what I just wrote runs counter to most owners' beliefs. But think about it for a moment—Books and Practices often depend on a single or primary individual who attempts to serve as the head of client services, marketing and sales, HR, IT, and so on. At some point, such an individual will simply *run out of gas*, or *hit a ceiling*, or whatever metaphor you would prefer. It is inevitable. Regardless, by age 55 or so, most founders who are still *forces of one* start to enjoy the results of their hard work and they begin to slow down and, justifiably, work less hard than they did in their thirties and forties. They can coast for a while, but eventually growth will suffer.

The building of an investable Business supports, even demands, a gradual shift from a *force of one* growth model to a complete team, carefully assembled one person at a time, one investor at a time, one expert in their field at a time, for decades over multiple generations of ownership. Theoretically, well run, growing Businesses are immortal... and that is part of why they're investable. Practically, we will just focus on a generation or two at a time and call it good.

G2 and G3 owners, or prospective owners, I urge you to always start your thinking about growth and change in terms of the Business's future trajectory. For example, using a 10% CAGR means that over 15 to 20 years, a common succession planning timetable, the Business you're investing in, with your help, will change significantly. Your Business will double in size, at least twice at this growth rate, even given economic obstacles that might reduce growth to zero or negative for a year or two along the way. At the other end of this growth tunnel, your Business (from the perspective of the Successor Team who will eventually own a majority interest) may well have different clients with diverse needs, served by more staff members who need increased expertise to meet those needs. These are good problems to have.

Ask yourself the questions, "What will this business need when it is 2X in size? 4X in size?!" and plan accordingly, and then execute to that plan. Build for that Business starting today. Do you have the right people? What other talent sets will that new Business you are building and contributing to require, in order to continue growing, satisfying, and attracting new clientele? By this time, of course, most G1s will be on the sidelines or retired. This new Business is yours to build and sustain.

One common change that we often see in a multi-generational Business results from the **Age Proximity Rule**. This rule or guideline suggests that clients and service providers (such as insurance professionals, financial advisors, accountants, doctors, therapists, or consultants) are often within a ten-year age range of each other, easing the process of trusting, communicating, and understanding one another. Effectively, with a good plan, G2 and G3 will be able to positively change a Business's client demographics by working with clients within their own ten-year age range (plus or minus), effectively regenerating and re-energizing the client base.

And know that slower growth can still support a Succession Plan, though it will have an effect on value and how investable the opportunity is perceived to be. Founding owners who struggle to maintain strong growth in their fifties or sixties often look to the succession planning process for a solution. Growth will be uneven, but with a good plan and generations of motivated talent to make it happen, it feels almost inevitable.

In the end, growth is what next generation owners who make an Equity investment depend on to support their purchase decision and to service their debt. Top-line growth channeled through an efficient cash flow system into bottom line profitability increases the Equity value over time. To make it all work, the top line of the P&L, or the gross revenues, have to grow. And the responsibility for such growth must be shared by all owners, young and old, and fully transfer at some point from the G1 level to the Successor Team (G2/G3) members. This is what it takes.

SECTION 2: UNLOCKING GROWTH: SCALING A PROFESSIONAL SERVICES BUSINESS

As the Business you are investing in grows and adds owners, the ability to scale it becomes increasingly important, and possible. Accept that it may well be your generation of ownership, G2/G3, who figures it out. If you are fortunate and smart about it, G1 and G2/G3 owners can at least start the process together and develop a strategic plan. Rarely have I seen G1, alone, figure out the scalability issue before taking on new, next gen owners.

A handful of G2 and G3 PSP owners know this stuff, but most do not, so let's address the basics first. Growth and scale are different issues. Most efforts to grow a Business are focused primarily on top line growth while watching overhead expenses (Basket No. 1) carefully with the goal of maintaining a certain level of profitability. But, typically, increasing the gross revenue of a Professional Services Business means increasing the expenses as well, often proportionally. **Scalability,** or **Scale,** is about growing the gross revenues disproportionately to the general overhead expenses of the Business. It requires planning, funding, the right systems and processes, staff, technology, and partners. This can be hard to do in a Professional Service model, but it is possible with a good plan and some high-level thinking.

The issue of Scale usually first arises when the strategies used in the past to grow a Practice or Business stop working, or at least stop working efficiently. Most entrepreneurs (G1s) reach a point where they simply can't work any harder or longer, and they cannot acquire and serve more clients. It feels like they need to expand the Business, but any more growth feels impossible to sustain. At some point, there is just too much to do and not enough hours in the day to get it done. The common solution? Hire and train another person to do exactly what the founder and chief revenue producer does. And then owners do that over and over again.

The common result is that most Professional Service Businesses do not become more profitable (as a percentage of gross revenue) as they get bigger. In the financial services and wealth management industries where I worked, for instance, benchmarking data is clear that profits on a percentage basis do not grow larger as revenues increase from $1,000,000 to $20,000,000—there is no material difference in overhead expenses or profitability for businesses in this range. They just get bigger.

Scale can be very elusive and I think the problem, especially in the Professional Services area, lies in entrepreneurial thinking, the very thing that helps every new owner survive in the early years of a new venture. As an entrepreneur, the first problem G1 has to solve for is revenue. If G1 can't make a living, their Book or Practice won't survive. But over time, an entrepreneur's confidence grows and the myriad challenges and problems are solved using ingenuity, hard work, even some trial and error. At some point, however, problems like figuring out how to scale a business surpass one's basic entrepreneurial skills; working harder is actually part of the problem. I can attest to this from personal experience coming from a long line of workaholics and entrepreneurs.

Here are some suggestions to consider and to talk to your fellow owner(s) about when the time is right. First, growth is a common theme in a sustainable business, so apply the concept to the issue of adding scale. The challenge is immediate, but the solution is not—it will take time, perspective and skill. As we began to explore in the previous Section, if your Business can sustainably grow at a 10% CAGR, in seven years it will double its revenue flow. So start now and scale *for that business*. Who will you need? What needs to change? What is missing? Start answering those questions now and lay out a plan and grow into it. Building for succession will provide a number of important guideposts along the way and require some new thinking and some new talent.

Second, in your owners' meetings, memorialize the group's goals and get specific about what you want or need to achieve and the timetable for doing so. And then read, learn, and listen. Hire a coach with a proven record in helping other Businesses like yours turn this corner. Consider hiring the talent you may not have and bring in new and better thinking on this subject matter. Study other businesses, even from other professions and industries (benchmarking is covered later in this Chapter). Working harder isn't the answer to the question so get smart about it.

Third, marketing and sales are common pinch-points for one-owner Practices that want to grow into valuable, profitable, sustainable Businesses. This is because at the Book and Practice levels of ownership, the entrepreneur does it all and starts to honestly believe that they are the best and only solution to obtain more clients and produce more revenue. I know I did. Many Practice owners, *forces of one*, think the answer lies in this approach: *Find another one of me. I am very good at what I do. Let's just keep doing what works. And if I can't do that, then I've grown as large as I can.* Hiring experienced marketing and sales professionals and arming them with goals and a budget dedicated to bringing in new clients and a high level of annual growth is a step forward in the Scalability process.

Fourth, building an Equity-Centric Business model provides unique tools to help Scale a business. Think back to Chapter Two, *Where Does the Money Come From to Buy In?* As the business grows, Equity can and should play a bigger part in the lives of more key employees and PSPs. Base compensation (wages + bonus) as the reward for work performed should yield to the benefits of Equity and Shareholder Value–the idea is to have more PSPs become owners and build wealth through Equity. Again, in a multi-owner, multi-generational Business, the cumulative salaries of the ownership team are one of the largest expenses a Professional Service model has, if not *the* largest. Stabilize owner's compensation for the entire team of owners (Basket No. 2), using profit distributions and stock appreciation in a growing Business as the better reward and incentive, increasing profitability directly and indirectly (using the Plateau Level Compensation System explored in Chapter Two, Section 3) . That is another step in the right direction of scaling a Business.

Finally, a common refrain that I like to apply to skeptics on this subject is to build a business that allows leaders to lead, let's professionals deliver professional services, marketing people market, and sales people sell. When you think about it, it really doesn't make sense to ask a highly trained, perhaps licensed and regulated service provider to also sell and market themselves within a Business. Isn't the best use of a professional's time found in delivering professional services to as many clients as possible? A Business leader's job is to figure out how to Scale the Business as it evolves and grows and the world changes around it. You simply cannot continue to do things the same way and expect different results, but you also cannot make these adjustments to an existing Business quickly or suddenly.

You might note that Scalability is not listed as one of the key attributes of an Equity-Centric Business. Not all Professional Service owners agree that it is necessary or even possible. I agree that bigger solves a lot of problems for Business owners and investors, but bigger is not the same as better. Working towards Scalability will make a Business better, in this generation or the next.

SECTION 3: PUTTING THE "M" BACK IN "M&A"

This section is about super-charged growth, and pushing the boundaries of growing a Business in every sense of that word. A statutory merger is a powerful growth tool to consider; it goes beyond an acquisition. Consider this case study. There are two G1s (G1(A) and G1(B)) both in their early sixties and each is an equal owner. There are no key employees ready to step in as G2s or G3s. The Business has done well and its value is approximately $3.0 million. The younger of the G1 owners (G1(B)) anticipates retiring earlier than his colleague, hopefully in about five years or fewer. G1(A) does not want to buy out G1(B) and take on the debt service. For the moment, they have reached an impasse on what to do next.

An interesting possibility to consider here is to attempt to merge a similar but smaller and younger group of owners into this Business and jump-start the Succession Plan with two or more G2's (G2(A) and G2(B)) who have ownership experience and who will become immediate owners upon completing the merger. This *coming together* may be a statutory merger when the two entities are corporations, or it may be an asset contribution when the continuing entity is an LLC taxed as a Partnership. Those are details that are best left to an M&A attorney and/or skilled accountant once a strong mutual interest in finding a solution exists, but there is usually a way, legally.

Continuing this case study, assume that G2(A) and G2(B) are also equal partners. Both are in their late thirties. They agree to merge their $1.5M appraised Business into G1's(A & B) $3.0M appraised Business. As a result, the new, post-merger ownership structure might look like this on a Tranche-by-Tranche basis (see *Figure 18*):

		Post-Merger		T1		T2		T3	
		Equity Levels		Equity Levels		Equity Levels		Equity Levels	
G1(A):		33%		25%		10%		0%	
G1(B):		33%		25%		0%		0%	
G2(A):		17%		25%		45%		45%	
G2(B):		17%		25%		45%		45%	
G3(A)								10%	

Figure 18

Within a year or two of the merger, T1 should occur, with T2 about four or five years later. G2(A) and G2(B) will not need a long-term bank loan to buy-in during T1, T2 and T3 because they have equity ownership via the merger with no debt to service and this will allow them to use, for example, up to 25% of the total profit dollars, each, to pay for an 8% acquired Equity Interest in T1, and then 45% of the total profit dollars, each, to pay for a 20% acquired Equity Interest in T2, and so on. This provides an acceleration effect using the Profit-Based Note theory covered previously. At some point, G3 buys out G1(A)'s remaining Equity Interest.

To make this work, all four of the original merger partners will probably need to be on the Business's Board of Directors with one vote per Director. Practically, they would each want a say in the Business's operations and governance structure.

On day one, post-consolidation, the Business is worth at least $4.5M and will have a good, diverse team of owners in place. G1(A) and G1(B) could also use a Residual Equity strategy, covered in Chapter Two (Section 8), as another possibility.

Obviously, a restructuring like this changes everything, for everyone. These are not easy to do, and compatible, long-term partners are not easy to find, but they offer possibilities and opportunities that neither of the smaller Businesses may have on their own. It just might be worth striving for and hiring a headhunter to compile a short list of prospects and getting to work on it.

SECTION 4: BENCHMARKING (AGAINST THE RIGHT BUSINESSES)

Another good title for this section would be: *Never stop learning, improving, borrowing, and sharing.* That is what benchmarking is all about. Some Professional Service venues have more data available and some venues will have that data better organized than others—still, learn what you can learn by studying any and all benchmarking data you can find. Coaches and coaching, addressed in the Section immediately following, can be a great source of such information or studies.

People, and certainly successful Professional Service Providers, love to share what they know and what they have learned. I think that we so willingly share information as owners because most of us borrowed the ideas or information from someone else on our way up! This is a chance to give back and to teach others in our chosen profession.

Business benchmarking data can be invaluable, but you have to determine where the information is coming from, how it was collected, and how it is being presented. It matters *who* is telling you *what*. Thinking back to Chapter One, if I were a young, new owner of a Practice and I'm working hard to figure out which end is up, I need to look no further than similarly situated Practices that are my relative size, and also those that are about twice my size. I would study the data, compare it to my fact pattern, learn what I could and make a plan to improve.

Sometimes, however, benchmarking data is a massive collection of information from anyone and everyone - young practitioners and old, Book owners and Business partners - and what you get is an average. The information is interesting, but mostly useless. And therein lies the problem with benchmarking data. Comparing notes is fun. But it is so easy to draw incorrect conclusions or to steer a path that seems so obviously right, only to find out that you're on the wrong path five years later and your better informed competition is passing you by. This underscores the high value of well-collected data sets and the proper presentation and analysis of that data. Oftentimes, state or national trade associations or guilds, for your specific Professional Service, can be good sources of such benchmarking or performance data.

The point is, don't reinforce incorrect thinking such as, "Look, I'm doing everything as well or better than my peers! I am going to stay the course with a few minor improvements." In the preceding Chapters and Sections, we discussed the process of building a profitable, valuable, growing, investable, and sustainable Business. To this end, you may well be contemplating building or contributing to something vastly different from what most owners have or will ever build. If you benchmark against what all the other one-owner, non-scalable, one-generational Practices are doing, you will simply learn what everyone else is doing in the process of failing to build a real Business. It isn't that a crowd doesn't have some wisdom to share, you just have to be sure that you're not looking at the wrong crowd.

I have always found that, for most professionals, the best way to compare notes and learn what really makes a difference in your business life is to join a study group. If you can find a group of eight to ten Business owners in your community, or who are willing to get together once a year off-site somewhere to meet for a day or two and compare notes and details and to explore new ideas and ways of thinking, grab the opportunity with both hands. Assemble the group if you have to but do not try to be the smartest person in the group or the largest business. Set any ego you might have aside. This is the chance to learn, improve, borrow and share…and to ask a lot of questions of successful peers! And then to make your own plans.

SECTION 5: WORKING WITH A COACH AND/OR MENTOR

One of the primary benefits of participating in a Succession Plan as a G2 or G3 owner is that the Equity opportunity comes with a built in mentor, or set of mentors, at the G1 ownership level. For certain, at least by our standard definitions, G1 is older and has a lot more experience. G2, you will probably be the first of a group to invest and to be mentored, and then to serve as mentor for the next generation in the same Business.

Mentoring and **Coaching** are both methods for developing people, but through different means. You don't have to choose between the two methods; do both. And I mean that sincerely. If self-improvement and professional improvement are among your goals, and as next gen PSPs they should be, you will benefit from utilizing both mentors and coaches in your life, for years and decades, not weeks or months.

Mentoring is about personal and professional development. In my experience, it is more personal than collaborating with your manager or supervisor, and it is centered on you, your abilities, and maybe even your weaknesses or shortcomings—similar to talking with a beloved Aunt or Uncle who listens carefully, and patiently, and then offers honest feedback and support afterwards. Maybe that isn't everyone's experience, but I remember my favorite mentors in the legal and regulatory professions quite fondly. These were great experiences and not easily replicated. And I didn't hire these people; they came with the job.

There is no set list of what this interaction might entail, nor even the duration, and that's part of the magic. I have always thought of mentoring as centered on "higher level issues" such as career challenges, struggles with other professionals or staff members in the office, work-life balance, sharing second thoughts about actions I'd taken, and such. A good mentor just seems to always be there; I never had to set an appointment. Sometimes they found me and just knew enough to ask the right questions. The qualities I gained from my handful of mentors made me a better person and, in turn, a better professional—but in that order. I think that with the coaches I've worked with, the order is just the opposite, and needed to be.

Coaches have a different skill set and a different focus, and they are hired for a different purpose, often for a limited and specific duration. They tend to be focused on developing set skills and identifying problems and solutions that impact you as a professional. Coaching is more performance-driven and focused on achieving specific goals through a consistent, scheduled series of meetings or sessions, for compensation.

A good coach, hired to address a specific problem or address a specific need, can be one of the most important professionals you will ever hire. Armed with experience and expertise, coaches can help you solve one or more difficult problems, often after you have spent years trying to solve them yourself. Most coaches will allow you to co-create the coaching agenda which could be personalized or tailored to a small group. A coach will often help frame and write out the specific outcome(s) desired. I find that the best coaches offer targeted assistance to address specific challenges.

In terms of cost, mentors are built-in to the Business in most cases. Coaches are hired. G2/G3, if I were thirty-something again and wanted or needed to improve at something important to my work, I would not hesitate to ask my partners or my supervisor to hire or provide a business coach for me. Be specific about what you need and what you want to accomplish, and how it will benefit the business. If they say "No," I'd rethink my request and come back and ask again a month or two later, and I'd keep asking.

G2, you do not need to wait until you're sixty years of age to mentor the next generation owners; in fact, you may well be much more effective than G1 given your younger age and more recent experiences on the ownership track. There is no age requirement or constraint, however, to this relationship-based transfer of knowledge. The concept of bi-directional mentoring includes younger PSPs mentoring older PSPs as well, especially on issues such as digital marketing, social media, and insights on a younger client demographic and how to reach them, among others. Help whenever and wherever you can, G2/G3, and support the flow of information and knowledge in the direction of the surrounding generations. You're all in this together.

SECTION 6: DEVELOPING A NICHE AND A SPECIALTY

As an older, somewhat successful guy, I like younger folks to get specific about their skills and knowledge base during our consulting work together. Do not tell me you offer great customer service. What, specifically, do you do better than anyone else? Don't tell me you have no peers in your profession or are just better—why? What skills? What peers are you referring to? Who else has made such an evaluation? Show me the evidence. Show me the opinions in writing. Everything else is just, well, air. And bags of air do not last long and they are not worth much. So let's get specific.

I like to think of a **Niche** as client-centered, the point being that you serve a unique group of clients in terms of their age, their trade, their geography, their struggles, their income level, etc. A **Specialty** is PSP-centered; it is about your unique skill set or body of knowledge. Obviously the two concepts are related and can overlap—having a specialty makes it easier and more likely that you will create a niche, but they still refer to different matters. Here is a more specific example to explain the differences and how they often complement each other.

About twenty years ago, when I was still figuring out my own craft, I took a call from a financial advisor who wanted to sell his niche practice for a premium. He was a former airline pilot who retired early and became a financial advisor and planner for other retired pilots of the same airline. He spoke the language. To this end, this advisor also created a digital newsletter (when such an approach was not yet common) about financial planning that was written to and about the unique retirement world of the professional pilot. Since this group tended to scatter around the country, if not the world upon career end, this single advisor used technology to follow them anywhere and deliver needed information everywhere. He built a niche Practice, and it paid off handsomely.

Less than ten years into this venture, this *force of one* Practice owner decided to retire himself and sell what he'd built along with its strong potential for growth and future earnings when expanded to other airlines and their retired pilots. He argued that a larger advisory firm with a strong marketing group could do so much more with this Niche than he could. He was right. He received a dozen great offers, and the practice sold within days at premium value—the highest I had ever seen at the time. This advisor worked with the buyer for about a year, seamlessly passing off both his Niche client base and his knowledge, his Specialty, to the new advisory firm who hired and trained several former airline pilots to replace him and build out the Niche.

G2 and G3 owners and ownership prospects, obviously you would need to apply these concepts to your unique Professional Services venue and figure out your own path. Of course there will be differences, but the take away here is that you are never too young to begin to figure out your specialty and hone that part of your own craft. Being great at something enables you, even as a younger, next gen owner or ownership prospect to bring important skills and knowledge to the table. An expert is someone who knows more and more about less and less. Make that work for you, develop a Specialty, and create a Niche business that will serve you and your partners well for decades to come.

And understand that you don't have to be too creative here—your Specialty might be something that your business already does or something unique that you know based on your working or educational history. I once consulted with a Registered Investment Advisor (RIA) whose Ph.D. thesis (years earlier and on a different career path) focused on metallurgy. A decade and a new career later, this RIA then figured out how to relate his thesis to the durability and resilience of the world's financial markets and developed a brilliant marketing campaign around a concept that he could call his own.

Put in the time, do the extra research, hire a Coach and/or talk to your Mentor, and *own your piece of this puzzle.* And then get better and better at it every day. From there, you can figure out how to tie this Specialty you now hold to the services offered by others on your team, or you might even be able to apply this Specialty to a unique group of new clients and create a Niche of your own.

Lessons To Be Learned

- Multiple generations of motivated owners working together are capable of generating higher revenue growth over a longer period than a single, experienced but aging founder, or even a small group of similarly aged founding owners.

- Scale is about growing the top line disproportionately to the general overhead expenses of the Business.

- A statutory merger is a powerful growth and reshaping tool well worth considering; it goes far beyond an acquisition.

- Mentoring and coaching are both methods for developing people, but are still very different in terms of goals and methods. You do not have to choose one or the other; do both.

- A niche is client-centered, the point being that you serve a unique group of clients in terms of their age, their trade, their geography, their struggles, their income level, etc. A specialty is PSP-centered; it is about a unique skill set or body of knowledge one holds.

Defined Terms in the Order Presented in this Chapter

- CAGR (or Compound Annual Growth Rate)
- Rule of 70
- Rule of 72
- Age Proximity Rule
- Scalability/Scale
- Mentoring
- Coaching
- Niche
- Specialty

CHAPTER NINE:
ARE YOU READY TO
BE AN OWNER?

In my early twenties, I worked for a large, publicly traded company in the small Midwest town where I was born and raised. I thought this was my forever job which is how it seemed to work out for my older friends and relatives. I sold my time and effort, and this big company in turn helped me pay all of my bills and find a direction. I started to accumulate the things I wanted and needed, all on a high school education. Of the 600 people that worked in that building, only eight had a four-year college degree; different times.

I thought I had a lot of control over my future because I was an honest, hard-working, dedicated individual. I showed up on time, or early, every single day. I did not know what was coming around the corner in terms of that particular business or industry, but at that age I didn't know what I didn't know. I figured that if I didn't have this job, for whatever reason, I could find another one quickly and easily. I was confident to the point of arrogance due to all that I did not know or understand. I didn't ask a lot of questions. I just trusted those around me and those older than I was, did what they did, and assumed all would be well.

Around three years into my forever job, I recall walking to my car one Friday afternoon. I saw my boss, a respected long-time employee in his mid-fifties, sitting in his car in the big parking lot, crying. I learned that his thirty-year career had come to a sudden end resulting from some important downsizing initiative—I'd heard the rumors. He had no idea what he was going to do next or how he was going to tell his spouse. It was the most open and honest conversation we'd ever had. He was one of several dozen to go home early that afternoon, all wondering what came next. Most of them were sitting in that same parking lot staring blankly into the future. None of them saw it coming even if, maybe, they should have.

I decided then and there that I needed to know what was coming around the proverbial corner. Not being a part of the decision-making process, and not having any control didn't make me safer, it just made my life as an employee simpler and easier. The danger was always there, and the changes were always lurking; I just didn't know enough to worry or care. I wasn't ready to be an owner of anything at that time of my life, but I made a plan. From that moment on, I was going to have control over my future. I set a goal to go to college and then law school and then become a sole proprietor, and later a business owner. And I did just that.

G2/G3, there are some different ways, perhaps better ways, to accomplish the ownership goal and that's what we'll talk about in this Chapter as you explore your own opportunities.

SECTION 1: STARTING A BUSINESS VS. BUYING IN

One of the first M&A (Mergers & Acquisitions) terms of art my legal mentor introduced me to, in the midst of a difficult business acquisition I was helping a client with was, "Should you buy it or build it?" That's a good question to consider carefully, especially as the opportunities and obligations of a Succession Plan come into sharper focus. In many Professional Service venues, there are a wider array of choices to consider in terms of ownership:

- Do you build your own business from scratch?

- Do you acquire another's Book or Practice and begin to build on that acquisition?

- Do you build on top of the business where you currently

work and practice, acquiring Equity gradually over time as in a Succession Plan?

Let's start with, *build your own business from scratch*. If you're of the entrepreneurial mindset, or there is no opportunity at your current place of business, this is a serious consideration. It means you start your own Practice or, as I like to say in the Professional Services world, you *hang out your own shingle*. This is exciting stuff and I find myself smiling as I write this part—maybe that's my next book! This is what I did, and I'd like to say that I have no regrets. It is the right answer for some Professional Service Providers (PSPs). Looking back, I'm so glad that I had this experience.

At the same time, it was incredibly difficult and time consuming, and expensive in that with little revenue flow to depend on for the first few years and the fixed expenses of life, I (we, as my wife would interject) had to take on some debt to stay afloat. That made me work harder, study my craft at a tenacious level, and worry more. I was eventually successful financially, but I came to miss the lessons learned by working with, alongside or under someone with a lot more experience. I did find my own mentors, and I hired my own coach when I could afford it, and that really helped. But it often felt like I was "practicing" on a big stage in front of a live audience, occasionally muffing my lines and, frankly, that took a lot of courage and a short memory. I didn't know I had it in me until after I did it!

Looking back, I realize that I put myself and perhaps my clients at a significant disadvantage by not having the daily training and interaction and support of a law firm (complete with senior partners, junior partners, associates and paralegals). To this end, I think you need ten years of actual, hands-on experience to be fully competent in your chosen profession. One of my more seasoned mentors told me that, after the fact, and he was right. I thought that I could just work harder and learn faster on my own as a sole proprietor. I was wrong.

I progressed from building my own small law practice to starting and building my own Professional Services Business, also from scratch, so

I guess I didn't learn very fast. But it was what I knew to do and there was no such opportunity or business to join and build on. As a result of starting and running my own one-lawyer law practice, I learned that I was indeed more comfortable working with a larger support team than being completely on my own. I quickly set out to surround myself with all the talent that I lacked in my small law practice. I got that part right. We grew the business to 65 people and then I retired from it.

A faster way than building from scratch is by acquiring another PSP's Book or Practice. A Book of 200 to 250 clients might seem like an instant goldmine, but often, it is mostly a long list of clients who may or may not have been well served, or recently served. Sometimes there are some assets (furniture, equipment and fixtures) that come with it or via an assumable lease. You can and should pay for the Book contingently if at all possible and then add these assets to what you're building. If you do it right, it will help you grow faster and learn more. Many times, a retiring seller will offer to mentor you and help you figure things out for six months to a year, part time.

I've seen PSPs buy a dozen small Books over the course of a career. They often call it their "marketing plan." Once you've bought one practice and done it right, or wrong, the rest of the acquisitions are much easier and you're likely to do it over and over again if you can find the sellers. This is the process of Book buying and, of course, there is a specific set of risks and rewards to carefully consider. Here is a summary of the first two options:

Pros:

- Complete Control: You're the architect of your own destiny. You are the boss. It's yours!

- Innovation/Creativity: Build something entirely new un-hindered by past owners and their decisions.

- Potential for Disruption: Challenge the status quo and carve out a unique market position.

- Reward: The satisfaction of building something from the ground up, on your own, is incredible.

- Geography: You determine where to locate the business rather than inheriting a location and a lease.

Cons:

- High Risk: Failure rates for startups are high. You are responsible for every aspect, including funding, hiring, training, marketing, and operations.

- Uncertainty: Revenue streams can be unpredictable and uneven, especially in the early years.

- Time-Consuming: Building a successful business requires a lot of time and energy.

- Financial Strain: Self-funding or securing investment can be challenging and may require significant personal sacrifice. Leases of property and equipment require an obligation, initially without the cash flow to pay for it all.

The other choice for you to consider is buying an Equity Interest in an ongoing Business, perhaps and hopefully as part of a formal Succession Plan. There is a specific set of risks and rewards to carefully consider with this approach too:

Pros:

- Reduced Risk: Building on an established foundation minimizes or eliminates any startup risks.

- Established Client Base: Inherit existing clients as well as new, incoming clients, and the related revenue streams.

- Proven Business Model: Rather than building from scratch, you work to gradually improve existing systems and processes.

- Mentorship: Gain invaluable experience and guidance from a seasoned entrepreneur and owner or owners.

Cons:

- Limited Control: You may inherit existing challenges, limitations, and outdated approaches.

- Potential for Disagreement: Aligning your vision and goals with the existing owner or ownership can be difficult.

- Poor Client Demographics: The client base of the business may be mostly around G1's age with few, new, younger clients coming in.

- High Purchase Price: Buying into an established business often requires a significant financial investment and long-term debt.

- Limited Ability to Innovate: You may be constrained by the existing business model and client base.

With eight previous Chapters to make the case, I'll leave it at that. The point is, consider all your options and make your own decision. In ten years or so, you'll know exactly what the right choice was.

SECTION 2: A MODERN DAY APPRENTICESHIP

As I worked through this second book of my Succession Planning series for Professional Service owners, it occurred to me that the training and development of younger professionals today shares some key characteristics with traditional apprenticeship models. One of the key themes in my books is to build on the foundations of knowledge, work and experience from a prior generation. So, how does one generation best transfer a career of knowledge, skills, and experience to the next generation?

G2/G3, one of my mentors was fond of saying that the only things we don't know is the history we haven't learned. Looking back, we all grew up learning about **Apprenticeships** in grade school, and how such *focused and guided learning* positively impacted our lives many generations later. Benjamin Franklin started as a printer's apprentice with his older brother, who laid the foundation for his career in publishing and his many other accomplishments. Paul Revere apprenticed as a silversmith, a trade that provided him with valuable skills and a network of contacts that would later prove crucial during the American Revolution. And George Washington apprenticed as a surveyor, learning land measurement, mapmaking, and other skills that served him well throughout his life, particularly in his military career.

Historically, most apprenticeships were tied to a trade or a craft. Traditionally, after completing an apprenticeship, a young person had a couple of options:

- The most common path was to become a journeyman which means that, effectively, they earned a wage working for someone else and honing their craft over the length of their career.

- Some apprentices, after accumulating enough savings and experience, would set up their own shop, becoming independent craftsmen or artisans.

- In fewer, even rare cases, apprentices could succeed their master (a term used in historical context and respectfully so), and potentially become a partner or even inherit or acquire the business.

Succinctly, apprenticeships of old were a method to source and train younger talent, and possibly to retain that talent. I acknowledge that, depending on the era, geographic location, and trade, apprenticeships of generations past could be brutal by today's standards. In the past 100 years or so, however, federal regulations here in the U.S. have changed this landscape and, today, apprenticeships are actually increasing in number and expanding into white-collar professions such as health care and information technology.

While traditional apprenticeship models may have originated in the trades, the core principles of structured learning, mentorship, coaching, and on-the-job training to develop practical, transferable skills are being effectively adapted by Professional Service owners today. In fact, the options and preferred, common pathways taken by next generation Professional Service Providers upon completing their training or on-the-job learning, really haven't changed a lot in 250 years!

The point of my two books in this Succession Planning series is to help make the case for today's apprentices, in whatever Professional Services venue they might work, to become a partner and/or acquire the business where they work and learn. I firmly believe that one generation working with and teaching the next, directly and as a career path, is the best way to improve the service professions and, therefore, the results their clients receive in the end.

The glue that binds the generations today, however, is Equity—the ability of a next generation apprentice to acquire a stake in the business where they work and learn. This is the difference maker! This gradual transfer of ownership echoes the gradual and continual transfer of knowledge, skills and experience from one generation to the next. Equity turns a transfer of knowledge from one generation to the next into a career-length investment by both teacher and student, or mentor and mentee. And with Equity comes a return on that investment if everyone works together, works hard, and works smart.

I do appreciate the entrepreneurs in the middle group who set up their own shop and begin anew, but having experienced that model as an entrepreneur myself, and as a client over the past 40 years or so, I do not think that is the best path to excellence and steady, meaningful improvement and growth of a services business. I think a multi-generational practice is much better situated to provide great service and continuing service, and a complete transfer of knowledge and skills, than a sole proprietorship model.

The modern adaptation of an apprenticeship for professional service owners lies in the form of a Succession Plan, which also provides the opportunity to continue the work within the same firm and eventually take over. It cannot remain among the "few, even rare cases" for a next generation service provider. With Equity as part of the tool set, it won't.

SECTION 3: DEALING WITH ACQUISITION DEBT

Debt is a natural part of business life, and it applies to launching a new venture as a sole proprietor, to buying Books and growing through one or more acquisitions, or buying an Equity Interest from a G1 owner. But in a practical sense, each of these debts feel quite different. Here are the important aspects from someone who has experienced all three.

Building from the ground up and becoming the owner of your own Book or Practice isn't really as much about managing debt as it is about managing your personal finances. The steady W2 paychecks and benefits of previous employment give way to possibilities and potential, as well as uneven cash flow—and a Practice that has a voracious appetite for any cash generated even as you need some take home pay. As long as you plan and save up for the experience, these issues can be mitigated. If you can, set yourself up with a Line of Credit and/or both a credit card and a charge card with as high a credit limit as possible, while you are still gainfully employed. You will also enjoy some tax savings or efficiencies in starting and growing a new Practice, but it may take years for cash flows to even out, to steady your take home compensation and to enjoy some predictability going forward.

Growth through acquisition is exciting. Each deal effectively stands on its own and, hopefully, the acquired cash flow covers the debt service. A good way to get started is with Seller Financing using some type of an earn-out approach, or an adjustable promissory note, if the seller is willing. An **Earn-Out Approach** is a formal, contracted payment structure that requires you to pay out, for example, 30% of every dollar you receive from the acquired clients for a period of three, four or five years typically, after a down payment and depending on a number of factors. If more money comes in from those acquired clients, then more money is paid out; if less money comes in for any reason, then less money is paid out to the seller. The final sum of money actually paid by a buyer to a seller equals the final value of the acquired Book and reflects the ultimate success of the transaction over time.

Alternatively, and perhaps more likely, you'll need to sign a promissory note with either the seller, individually, or a bank, conventionally. Sellers tend to offer up to five-year terms and banks tend to offer five to seven-year terms, maybe as long as ten years on an SBA-backed loan. Regardless, the goal, if all goes according to plan, is to service the debt from the acquired cash flow. Another contingent payment option is to use an **Adjustable** or **Performance-Based Promissory Note**. These note structures essentially have a look-back provision, often one year after the acquisition is closed, or completed. If only 82% of the acquired and promised cash flow transfers, then the Note is reduced by 18% and locked in place no matter what happens after this onetime adjustment. There are many other ways to structure such a note as well.

One major advantage is that as a buyer of assets, you can write off and/or depreciate the entire purchase price over time, albeit fifteen years in most cases. It does not matter how the acquisition is financed–if you acquire assets as opposed to stock or equity. Having watched many buyers acquire multiple Books or Practices, you are advised to leave about two to three years minimum between each acquisition to learn and adapt, and to ensure that you have the infrastructure to handle the sudden group of new clients and that you're acquiring, and hopefully retaining.

Acquiring an Equity Interest is different once again from the other approaches. Most G2s and G3s buy in, Tranche by Tranche, or incrementally as the Business grows. This means that not only does each Equity purchase get more expensive, each Equity purchase is with after-tax dollars, so, practically, add about 30% to 35% to the purchase price depending on your location and tax bracket, and reread the Section on Basis in Chapter Two. Each Equity purchase (with the possible exception of T1) tends to be conventionally financed for up to ten years and most Tranches overlap. Still, if you acquire a 10% interest in each of three Tranches (10% x 3), each with separate, conventional loans, this works out to about fifteen to twenty years of debt service. It might be less if the Business is growing fast and consistently, and the profit distribution dollars are increasing in amount and as a percentage of gross revenue, but it still takes time. Buying Equity, or stock, in this manner is a long-term, slow process that relies on the business cash flow machinery (i.e., your profit distribution dollars in a growing Business) to make it work.

Why buy Equity and go into debt for up to twenty years? We'll go back to the basic answer, which is Shareholder Value, or "what's in it for you, G2/G3?":

WAGES + PROFIT DISTRIBUTIONS - DEBT SERVICE + STOCK APPRECIATION

...over that full twenty-year period, all the while partnering to grow the Business and solve problems along-side your fellow owners. You are part of a team. Toward the end of that same twenty-year period, this is what the formula looks like as the tables turn in your favor:

WAGES + PROFIT DISTRIBUTIONS + EQUITY INCOME + STOCK APPRECIATION

And if you choose to Seller Finance your first sale of Equity, add Interest to the formula as well. Of course, Businesses cost more to buy, or buy into, than a Book or a Practice and that is because, in most cases, Businesses have greater revenues and profits, and a much higher value for good reason. In determining which model makes the most sense, fall back on doing the math and compare the numbers for yourself. If you have a mentor, it never hurts to have an objective opinion on your spreadsheet work, your plans, and your optimism.

SECTION 4: IS SYNTHETIC EQUITY A BETTER ALTERNATIVE?

Let's start with a basic fact: Equity ownership in a small business isn't for everyone. Add in the notion of a ten-year amortized, personally guaranteed conventional bank loan to service the debt for a minority interest, and Equity ownership in a small business narrows to a select group.

Synthetic Equity is a way to provide you with some of the economic benefits of ownership without your buying actual stock, or Equity. The more common terms associated with this concept include phantom stock, stock appreciation rights (SARs), a long-term incentive plan (LTIP), or a profits interest.

Synthetic Equity, in all its various forms, tends to offer key employees "ownership like benefits" without the attendant debt obligations. The catch is that you will be required to contribute your best efforts in helping the Business grow and/or achieve specific objectives; and you *need to be there* when the reward payment is made or due, making tenure part of the quid pro quo. Meanwhile, actual Equity is reserved for those investors who are willing and able to bear the risk of buying in to ownership.

Briefly, here is an illustration of how Synthetic Equity works (see *Figure 19*):

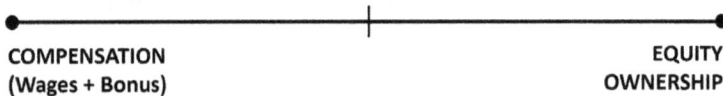

COMPENSATION   **EQUITY**
(Wages + Bonus)   **OWNERSHIP**

Figure 19

On the far left of this line, or spectrum, think of a traditional W2 base wage or salary plus a variable or discretionary bonus paid quarterly or annually based on metrics agreed upon by employer and employee. On the far right, think generally of shares of stock in Newco, LLC ("Newco"), electing to be taxed as a Partnership or an S-Corporation, and specifically of a G2/G3 owner who buys a 10% Equity Interest in Newco. Effectively, everything in between the left dot and the right dot is where Synthetic Equity exists or can exist if ownership is so inclined and creative enough.

Synthetic Equity is something less than Equity ownership with all its attendant benefits and obligations, and it is something more than a base wage plus a bonus. That's a lot of territory to work with. In the hands of a skilled plan designer, Synthetic Equity can take on more of the compensation elements, or more of the equity-based elements, leaning right or leaning left on this diagram.

More specifically, owning stock in a small business provides you as a G2 or G3 owner or investor with a *bundle of rights* that include a voice in the governance and operations, Cost Basis, a share of profit distributions, stock appreciation benefits, limited liability, the ability to sell the Equity at LTCG tax rates less Basis, and more. What many PSPs don't realize is that this bundle of rights is severable. Synthetic Equity often works with only one or two of these rights and fashions a tax-compliant, motivational, long-term benefit or compensation package for one or more key employees, or G2/G3 prospects.

To be clear, a Succession Plan requires next generation owners to make an actual investment in Equity ownership, often a career-length obligation, and there is no substitute for that. Accordingly, G1s, G2s and G3s exist to the far right of this spectrum. Synthetic Equity typically plays no role in obtaining and/or paying for Equity in a Business unless it provides for convertible interests earned synthetically—not a common feature in most Succession Plans.

We're introducing this concept to you as a G2 or G3 prospect because you do have a choice. In addition, there is no better substitute for treating key employees like owners–whether that's you, or an individual who one day works for you–and providing needed recognition and monetary rewards to keep the entire team together in support of a valuable, profitable, and sustainable Business.

One last point, regulatory bodies often govern the eligibility of Equity ownership in many Professional Service Businesses. Synthetic Equity can be a great alternative for the non-licensed staff members who really make a difference and whose Length of Service (LOS) deserves consideration of something more than the basic wage and bonus reward system. Depending on the underlying entity structure, Synthetic Equity can offer a vast array of tools to work with. LLC's taxed as Partnerships offer the widest array of options, but even a basic S-Corporation provides good, reliable Synthetic Equity choices as well.

SECTION 5: DEALING WITH BUY-IN DOCUMENTATION

As a G2 or G3 ownership candidate, you will need to perform Due Diligence on this investment opportunity. A major part of that process will involve carefully reading the existing document set as well as any newly drafted documentation for your Equity buy in.

In this Section, we'll provide an inventory of the typical document set you should expect to see as part of the underlying entity structure and for the first Tranche of ownership you might be involved in. Formal business valuations will also be necessary whenever stock is bought, sold, or financed and that is a document to study thoroughly. If a bank is involved, that lending source will issue their own additional document set, which are not included in the following lists. Starting with the entity structures:

Newco, LLC/Partnership:

- Articles of Organization
- Operating Agreement
- Members Agreement (or Buy-Sell Agreement)
- IRS Form 8832 (Tax Election Form)
- IRS Form SS-4 (Employer Identification Number)
- Consent Resolutions
- Stock Transfer Ledger
- Initial and Annual Reports
- Trade name or ABN (Assumed Business Name)—if operating under a name different from that of the entity
- Name Reservation Application
- State and Municipal Registrations
- Local Business Licenses
- Employer/Payroll Registrations

There will be some variations given the city/county/state rules and regulations, and while this list isn't exhaustive, it is intended to help you understand what to expect and what to review for an LLC electing Partnership tax treatment.

S-Corporation:

- Articles of Incorporation
- Bylaws
- Shareholders Agreement (or Buy-Sell Agreement)
- IRS Form 2553 (to make a Subchapter S election)
- IRS Form SS-4 (Employer Identification Number)
- Consent Resolutions
- Meeting Minutes
- Stock Transfer Ledger
- Initial and Annual Reports
- Trade name or ABN (Assumed Business Name)–if operating under a name different from that of the entity
- Name Reservation Application
- State and Municipal Registrations
- Local Business Licenses
- Employer/Payroll Registrations

Pausing for a moment–why does all this matter as a G2 or G3 prospective owner if you can't change any of the documents or decisions and the entity is already set up and in operation? The answer is, because you need to read every single one of the operational and set up documents to learn and understand what you are investing in and how all the parts interact. Study well.

That is the basic document set for two of the most common entity structures. Next, let's go over the basic document list needed to begin an actual Succession Plan.

<u>Documentation for each owner to support Tranche One (T1) of a Succession Plan:</u>

- Non-Disclosure Agreement
- Due Diligence Checklist
- A Letter of Intent or Memo of Understanding (optional)
- Employment Agreement (optional)
- Contribution Agreement(s)
- Assignment & Assumption Agreement(s)
- Bill(s) of Sale
- Membership Interest Sale Agreement
- A Joinder Agreement (binding the buyer to existing governance provisions)
- Financing Documents (such as a Promissory Note and Security Agreement)

Note that this entire document set is of the "forever" variety, especially for next generation investors. Forget the basic rules about keeping legal documents or records for 5 to 6 years. Safeguard these documents for life. I can't tell you how many times I've gone back to my original documents, twenty years later, for some minute detail that matters for some obscure reason in our too complicated business and tax world. Plus, when the time comes to sell your Equity Interest, these documents are how you will prove how much Basis you have and can use to offset tax liabilities from a sale of Equity.

SECTION 6: CRITERIA FOR OWNERSHIP

G2 and G3, as an ownership prospect, you are expected to be Professional Service Providers or PSPs. Not every PSP, however, is or should be an owner. So who is ownership material and who is not? What are the specific criteria?

G2 and G3, you should be very good at your craft to be considered as a potential Equity partner. To this end, most G1s require that a G2/G3 prospect meet two basic criteria before considering anything else:

- Length of Service (LOS)
- Revenue production

To summarize a previous position taken in this book, a three-to-five-year LOS is fast for potential G2/G3 owners; Professional Service owners usually need four-to-six years. Once LOS has been met, production is the next hurdle and G1's revenue production is the benchmark next gen PSPs are measured against. How much consistent, annual revenue production is enough? That's up to G1. Regardless, I caution against using these two criteria as automatic qualifiers for ownership, but this is where most Business owners start.

Building on these basic criteria, next on the shortlist is character. I consistently urge G1s to look toward their prospective G2/G3's specific past behavior and experiences, good and bad, and not hearsay or rumors or office gossip. Together, revisit such episodes and talk about what lessons were learned with the benefit of hindsight and the passage of time. G2/G3, what would you do differently next time? How would you counsel the next generation to handle a similar issue or event? This is why LOS matters—this part of the evaluation process simply takes time, observation, and experience.

G2/G3, being an owner also means adding another level of skills to your portfolio, that of running or at least significantly contributing to the operations of the Business you're investing in. As a G1 owner who has hired and promoted a few G2/G3 owners, here is how I would think through the process of figuring out who the next owner will be. I would start with these questions of ownership candidates during a formal interview with all the founding owners participating:

- In addition to your professional service skills and production, how will you make our Business better?
- Do you see yourself as a future CFO, or COO, or CIO for the Business?
- What degrees or designations have you earned or are still seeking?

- How do you currently represent our company in the community, providing specific examples?

- Do you understand, or aspire to understand the financial aspects of this Business and how it benchmarks against its competitors, and where it could improve?

- Tell us about an idea you had to make this Business better during your time here...

- Can you contribute a unique Specialty?

- Are you developing or could you develop a Niche client base that will be valuable to the Business and your partners?

- Is management and leadership something you enjoy, or shun?

- Do you have a good work/life balance? What would you do differently as an owner?

- How do you empower your peers to be better at what they do?

- Are you willing to keep learning more? And to teach what you've learned?

Of course, after G1 works with you, G2/G3, for at least a couple of years, they will think they know the answers to most of these questions. But this is an exploration and a discussion, and your presentation skills under pressure matter. Use these questions to start a conversation. G2/G3, you should think about these questions and do some soul searching far in advance of the Equity interview. Why do you want to be an owner? How can you make a difference? There are no perfect owners or ownership candidates, but these factors are where it starts for me. And the answers, as you probably realize, begin to form on day one of your employment. I'd note that these questions and answers are even more interesting when Onboarding a new PSP from outside the Business!

The issue of LOS or tenure isn't just about spending enough time to learn your way around, it is also important on the criteria list because the founding generation needs to be sure of a future partner's intent, skills and willingness to go "all in." By that same measure, next generation PSPs, you need to be sure that you are willing and capable of making a career-length investment, in every sense of that phrase. That takes time to figure out and there isn't a shortcut.

Finally, I would want to consider and discuss your willingness and ability to incur the risk of ownership. Though we've explored the use of Seller Financing and explained that it almost always works because G1(s) can be as flexible as they need to be, this isn't always the best course. The goal isn't to make ownership easy, just possible and practical. G2/G3, you need to treat this like any other investment and financial commitment. It has risks and they are real. It is long term. You are personally responsible for the obligations. Share these concepts with your spouse or significant other because this investment will need their long-term support too.

Regardless of how a given Business chooses to memorialize its ownership rules or guidelines, the basics of this ownership opportunity should be shared verbally with all new PSP hires, perhaps as soon as the initial hiring interview. Equity ownership is important and powerful. G2/G3, in time, you will be the best communicators of "what it takes to be an owner" to the generations that follow because you will have had the full experience.

SECTION 7: WHEN G1 SAYS "NO" TO ADDITIONAL OWNERS

More than a few times in my consulting career, G1, individually or as a group of similarly aged founders, says "No" to admitting new, next-generation owners. Alternatively, the answer is "Yes," but for a relatively nominal amount of Equity (i.e., 5% or less) and with no promises or hint as to when, if ever, a G2 or G3 owner might acquire more.

Sometimes the issue centers on the specific person being considered for an Equity Interest, but more often the issue is tied to the underlying mechanisms of the process. G2/G3, here is a short list of the common concerns that often serve as the basis for a G1's reluctance:

- Dilution of the profit distribution dollars

- A change to the governance structure or voting power

- A preference to one day sell the business for maximum value to a larger, outside buyer

- The business valuation and the resulting stock price is too low

- Next generation's work ethic (or lack thereof)

- An obvious need for Seller Financing, and the unwillingness to provide it

- The thought of a Succession Plan as equivalent to G1's retirement or exit plan

- Resentment of G2/G3s buying in using business cash flows (i.e., profit distributions)

G2/G3, be ready to deal with this issue and any and all the underlying concerns whether accurate or not. As a consultant faced with this situation, I start by suggesting that both sides learn more about the Succession process—there are a lot of misconceptions. Of course, this is also why I author these books and why I wrote one specifically for G1, and this one specifically for you as a G2/G3 prospect. Read more. Learn more. Ask questions. Talk to each other.

I also strongly encourage the current owners and prospective G2 or G3 ownership candidate(s) to work through the math using a pro forma spreadsheet process. Do the math and make a decision from the facts. Building out a detailed, pro forma spreadsheet on an impending buy-in opportunity is essential before saying "Yes," or "No." A new owner will immediately lay claim to a share of the profit distribution dollars and stock appreciation rights and that will always be a concern, or an issue, at least in the short term. The modeling process needs to explore and explain how this affects each individual owner, current and future, in the long term (i.e., ten years or more in most cases). If "No" is still the answer after working through the numbers in detail, perhaps a specific reason may come to the surface that can be addressed.

A fallback provision may lie in the use of Synthetic Equity. I have worked with G1s who did want to sell the entire business within three to five years at the highest possible value. In such a situation–and where G2/G3 key employees made a meaningful difference–their loyalty was rewarded with an equity-like benefit. One example is for G1 to promise, in writing, 5% or more of the sales price, when and if that occurs, to entice the key employees to stay and help and improve the business value to the benefit of all.

And, sometimes, "No" means "No" and the only options are to stay and work and negotiate a better compensation package, or to walk away before investing any more time. This is why ownership should be discussed sooner than later, and often.

Before we close this Chapter out, let's talk about a fairly common approach that feels somewhere between a "No" and *death by a thousand cuts*. Several times now, I have listened to a G1 owner describe a self-constructed Succession Plan to sell or grant 1% of their Equity each year to a key employee up to 10% or some other number, and then figure it out from there. G1 commonly reserves the right to terminate this arrangement at any time. Sometimes, especially in a Stock Grant situation, G1 adds a caveat that the stock will not fully vest until year ten, or later, or upon G1's full retirement or a sale of the entire business.

In the 30 years of doing this, as an attorney and as a consultant, I have never seen this plan actually work. The problem is, G2/G3 usually says "No," or G2/G3 ends up leaving for a better opportunity a few percentage points into the process. By the way, stock that has not vested does not receive any profit distributions or stock appreciation benefits, and, when it does finally and fully vest, the value at the time of vesting is what G2/G3 will be taxed on, and at ordinary income rates, with a few exceptions that aren't material to this discussion. Aside from all the other issues and regardless of whether the 1% plan is a series of sales or grants, the real problem is that G2/G3 doesn't feel like an owner, at least not for the first five years or so, and really not until the stock vests. This approach is too slow, too cautious, and too impractical.

To be clear, the take away from this Section, G2/G3 reader, isn't how to get past "No," it is figuring out G1's ownership plans soon enough to do something about it one way or the other. So, start asking!

Lessons To Be Learned

- In terms of ownership criteria, tenure or production, or both, should not be the numerical and automatic determinants for an Equity buy in opportunity. There is far more to it than that.

- Debt is a natural part of business life, but it will significantly affect the decision whether to start your own practice, acquire a retiring owner's Practice, or buy an Equity Interest as part of a Succession Plan. All debt is not created equally.

- Synthetic Equity is a way to provide you with some of the economic benefits of ownership without your buying actual stock, or Equity, and taking on debt.

- The glue that binds the generations today is Equity—the ability of a next generation apprentice to acquire a stake in the business where they work and learn. This gradual transfer of ownership echoes the gradual and continual transfer of knowledge, skills and experience from one generation to the next.

- Whether there is, or is not, an ownership opportunity at the business where you work, it is best to know the answer as early as possible.

Defined Terms in the Order Presented in this Chapter

- Apprenticeships
- Earn-Out Approach
- Adjustable or
- Performance-Based Promissory Note
- Synthetic Equity

A CALL TO ACTION

Ownership of a small business is not for the faint of heart. So, perhaps it goes without saying, but don't be shy. If you aspire to ownership and it is an essential step in your future wealth building and professional development, say something. Do something about it.

My advice, and this may be more appropriate for G3, is to start the ownership discussion during your initial employment interview. Something like this: "Yes, I do have some questions, thank you. Do you have an ownership plan laid out for the future of this business? I'd like to have the opportunity to buy in as my career progresses and you see what I can do. Equity is important to me." Of course, you should also do your Due Diligence ahead of time. Does the business you're interviewing with have more than one owner? More than one generation of ownership? Are there family members involved in the day-to-day operations? Is it a Book, Practice or a Business? Maybe you'll be the first next gen owner, but it is also possible that the founder(s) plan to sell it to a third party and then you'll be starting all over, six or seven years down the road.

When and if you break through and become an Equity partner, I'd ask again: "Thank you for this opportunity. What is it, specifically, that you're looking for before I have a chance to buy additional Equity?" And then listen. It is OK if G1 doesn't have the answers. Just follow up and ask again in a couple of months and tell them that you will be doing that, to expect it, because it is important to you. If sharing ownership makes the founding owner(s) uncomfortable—again, you need to know. Silence and hope is not a plan.

As I wrote in the first book of this series, I am not here to sell you anything more than the advice and information in this book. My primary role is to organize the succession planning space for Professional Service Providers and help you figure out how to best move your ownership dreams forward. I also enjoy the teaching process. You can hire me as a consultant, or not, but that probably needs to run through G1 and the Business. So, ask them for help. Give them a copy of the book I wrote for the G1 ownership level, *Building With the End in Mind: A Complete Succession Planning Guide for Professional Service Owners.* Start a conversation. Perhaps there is an opportunity to speak about this subject at your annual conference if your profession has one—let me know. Glad to meet up afterwards.

If you need additional information or have questions, you would like to ask during or after you read this book, there is a website you can go to at:

www.ProfessionalServicesSP.com

There is no cost to use this website or to email your questions, or to read the blog posts. I welcome your continued involvement and interest. I anticipate posting new additions to this book, even corrections or adjustments when warranted, creating a dynamic reading experience through this website. Your questions and critiques will help me, help you, better understand the complexities and the myriad possibilities afforded by this subject matter, across a wide variety of Professional Service venues. Please stop by and say hello.

You can even set up a free 30 minute one-on-one appointment to confidentially talk about your specific situation and see if a Succession Plan and/or an ownership opportunity makes sense for you given your circumstances. To be certain, this book and its accompanying website are all about learning and exploring. Subscribe online at no cost using only your name and email address, confidentially of course.

Here is a specific action item list to help you get started:

- ☐ If you have made it this far and read all of *Acquiring Your Future Through a Succession Plan*, consider reading the key Chapters again a month or two from now—the details matter and you need to develop a mastery of the concepts and the terminology

- ☐ Subscribe at www.ProfessionalServicesSP.com and introduce yourself

☐ Use the "Ask Questions" tab or the "Schedule a Free 30-Minute Conversation" tab to start a conversation (feel free to invite G1 to join when you are ready)

☐ Share a copy of *Building With the End in Mind* with the current owner(s) and help them help you on this quest

Other action items to consider–as I wrote to the G1 owners in the other book, invest the time and money to have the Practice or Business objectively valued to see where it is at in terms of actual value. Like it or not, an objective, professional opinion provides needed information. From there, further develop the Plan by working with a Financial Analyst to blueprint your Succession Plan and work through the math. See where that takes you and the ownership team. As you read in Chapter Two, the math of a Succession Plan is often quite compelling, but that is not an absolute—and it is *a pro forma* spreadsheet. Perhaps the Practice or Business where you work needs some help in terms of organizing its cash flows, rethinking compensation strategies, and increasing profitability. I would be glad to offer you some suggestions and direction if you like.

Don't worry about figuring out all the answers at this point. It is enough to start a dialogue between the generations and to start asking the necessary questions. The answers will come in time.

The End

PostScript: If you enjoyed this book, please consider leaving an honest review at your favorite store or on-line book distribution center. I would appreciate it very much.

INDEX

A

Adjustable or Performance-Based Promissory Note: 188, 200

Age Proximity Rule: 165, 177

Apprenticeships: 184, 200

B

Board of Directors: 52, 63, 90, 122, 125, 126, 127, 130, 136, 170

Book building: 52, 63, 71, 73, 90, 122, 125, 126, 127, 130, 136, 170

Business Governance: 52, 63, 90, 120, 122, 125, 126, 127, 130, 136, 170

Business Legacy Model: 52, 58, 63, 73, 90, 122, 125, 126, 127, 130, 136, 170

Buy-Sell Agreement: 23, 31, 50, 61, 91, 93, 103, 115, 116, 117, 132, 138, 149, 157, 192, 193

C

CAGR: 113, 162, 163, 164, 167, 177

Capital Assets: 28, 29, 31, 33, 47, 76, 84, 86, 87, 89, 96, 114

Chief Executive Officer (CEO): 124, 125, 136

Chief Financial Officer (CFO): 124, 126, 136

Chief Operating Officer (COO): 125, 126, 136

Coaching: 173, 174, 177

Connelly vs. US, No. 23-146, 602 U.S. ___ (June 2024): 117, 118

Continuity Plan: 22, 23, 25, 27, 30, 31, 50, 61

Control Premium: 108, 118

Cost Basis: 191

  Basis: 191, 194

Cost of Living Adjustment: 43, 56

D

Drag-Along Rights: xi, 131, 133, 136

Due Diligence: 79, 86, 96, 111, 112, 113, 117, 139, 140, 149, 150, 192, 194, 201

E

Earn-Out Approach: 187, 200

EBITDA: 7, 104, 105, 107, 111, 118

Employer Identification Number (EIN): 79, 96, 192, 193

Equity Blueprint: ix, 36, 38, 56, 139

Equity-Centric Business: ix, 25, 26, 30, 31, 34, 40, 43, 66, 78, 162, 168, 169

Equity Income: 37, 45, 51, 52, 56, 105

Equity Interest or Equity: 31

Exit Plan: 21, 22, 23, 27, 30, 31, 36, 45, 100, 102, 104, 105, 107

F

Fair Market Value: x, 7, 27, 37, 56, 60, 103, 106, 116, 118, 119, 131, 138

Figure 1: 11

Figure 2: 26, 27

Figure 3: 28, 29

Figure 4: 34

Figure 5: 37

Figure 6: 38, 39

Figure 7: 40

Figure 8: 41

Figure 9: 42, 43

Figure 10: 48

Figure 11: 51

Figure 12: 59

Figure 13: 85

Figure 14: 86

Figure 15: 104

Figure16: 123

Figure 17: 124

Figure 18: 170

Figure 19: 190

Full Recourse Loan: 157, 159

G
G1/G2/G3: 12, 31, 128
Gifting Stock: x, 92, 97
Granting Stock: 97
Gross Revenue Multiple (or GRM): 118

H
Hybrid Model: x, 85, 86, 96

I
Internal Revenue Code (IRC): 18, 46, 56, 86, 97
Intrinsic Value: 103, 118
Investment Value: 103, 118
IRC §368: 87, 97
IRC §721: 97

J
Job/Book: 31

L
Length of Service (LOS): 49, 60
Life Insurance: x, 115
Limited Liability Company
  LLC/Partnership: 192
Long Term Capital Gains (LTCG): 56

M
M&A (Mergers & Acquisitions): xi, 70, 99, 134, 169, 170, 180
Members Agreement: 23, 31, 132, 133, 136, 192
Mentoring: 173, 177
Minority Discount: 106, 107, 108, 109, 118
Minority Interest: 106, 118, 119

N
Nepotism: 148, 159
Newco, LLC, or Newco: 27, 28, 29, 31, 33, 34, 35, 37, 46, 47, 86, 88, 89, 90, 91, 92, 93, 94, 95, 112, 114, 115, 116, 120, 128, 129, 132, 190, 192
Niche: xi, 175, 176, 177, 196
Non-Nepotism: 148, 159
Non-Recourse Note: 156, 157, 158, 159
Non-Voting Stock: xi, 130
Notate Bene or, Important Notes: 15, (11-14)

O
Onboard/Onboarding: 97

P
Performance Ratios: 41, 43, 56, 66, 73, 109, 110, 111, 135
Phantom Income: 91, 152, 159
Plateau Level Compensation Strategy: 42, 43, 56
Practice: 13, 23, 24, 25, 26, 28, 30, 31, 40, 48, 51, 65, 68, 70, 71, 72, 73, 81, 85, 87, 99, 101, 102, 105, 112, 140, 141, 143, 148, 149, 156, 161, 163, 164, 166, 167, 168, 171, 176, 180, 181, 182, 187, 189, 200, 201, 203
Price vs. Value: 107, 118
Profit-Based Note: 38, 40, 44, 56, 170

Q
Quarterly Estimated Tax Payments: 151, 159

R
Reasonable Compensation: 84, 96, 110
Residual Equity: x, 53, 54, 55, 56, 154, 171
Return on Investment (ROI): 56
Rule of 70: 163, 177
Rule of 72: 163, 177

S
Scalability/Scale: 177
S-Corporation: x, 19, 24, 27, 28, 51,

52, 67, 77, 78, 79, 80, 82, 83, 84, 85, 87, 88, 90, 96, 107, 110, 120, 128, 146, 150, 151, 190, 192, 193

Seller Financing: ix, 38, 40, 43, 44, 45, 46, 55, 56, 109, 116, 119, 138, 156, 157, 187, 197, 198

Shareholders Agreement: 31, 193

Shareholder Value: 19, 31, 45, 51, 55, 72, 112, 141, 145, 168, 189

Small Business Administration: 44

Specialty: xi, 175, 176, 177, 196

State and Local Taxes (SALT): 83

Stewardship Rules: 138, 139, 146, 154, 158, 159

Stock Redemption: 89, 91, 97, 112

Succession Plan: iv, ix, x, xi, 20, 21, 22, 23, 24, 25, 26, 27, 30, 31, 33, 34, 36, 45, 46, 47, 48, 50, 51, 52, 53, 54, 55, 57, 58, 59, 60, 61, 63, 64, 66, 67, 68, 69, 72, 75, 76, 77, 78, 80, 81, 82, 83, 87, 89, 90, 92, 94, 96, 100, 102, 103, 104, 105, 106, 107, 108, 114, 116, 117, 122, 129, 130, 132, 136, 139, 141, 143, 147, 153, 155, 156, 157, 165, 169, 173, 180, 181, 183, 186, 191, 193, 194, 198, 199, 200, 202, 203

Successor Team: x, 20, 21, 23, 25, 31, 35, 37, 47, 48, 49, 50, 52, 53, 54, 59, 60, 61, 62, 63, 64, 70, 72, 73, 86, 87, 92, 105, 107, 108, 119, 130, 132, 136, 141, 142, 143, 154, 164, 165

Support Team: x, 67, 68, 69, 72, 73

Synergistic Value: 103, 118

Synthetic Equity: xii, 62, 81, 189, 190, 191, 192, 199, 200

T

Tag-Along Rights: xi, 131, 132, 133, 136

Tax Conduit (or flow-through entity): 35, 41, 96

Tax-Neutral Exchange (TNE): 77, 84, 86, 96, 97, 114, 129

Tenure: x, 60, 62, 196, 200

The Basic Premise: 9,10,15

The Intended Audience: 5,6,7,15

Trailing 36 months (T-36): 118, 207

Trailing Twelve Months (T-12): 66, 101

Tranche One (T1): 37, 42, 45, 52, 56, 61, 68, 111, 128, 132, 157, 194, 207

Tranche(s): 31, 54

Tranche Two (T2): 37, 56, 61, 207

V

Voting Stock: xi, 130

W

www.ProfessionalServicesSP.com: 202

Y

Your Guide: 1,2,3

www.ingramcontent.com/pod-product-compliance
Lightning Source LLC
Chambersburg PA
CBHW071206210326
41597CB00016B/1686